T0120096

Welcome Home Healthy Cookbook

Welcome Home Healthy Cookbook

HEALING COMFORT FOOD RECIPES FOR YOUR SLOW COOKER, STOVETOP, AND OVEN

Hope Comerford

Good Books

New York, New York

Copyright © 2020 by Good Books, an imprint of Skyhorse Publishing, Inc.

Photos by Bonnie Matthews, Clare Barboza, and Getty Images

All rights reserved. No part of this book may be reproduced in any manner without the express written consent of the publisher, except in the case of brief excerpts in critical reviews or articles. All inquiries should be addressed to Good Books, 307 West 36th Street, 11th Floor, New York, NY 10018.

Good Books books may be purchased in bulk at special discounts for sales promotion, corporate gifts, fund-raising, or educational purposes. Special editions can also be created to specifications. For details, contact the Special Sales Department, Good Books, 307 West 36th Street, 11th Floor, New York, NY 10018 or info@skyhorsepublishing.com.

Good Books is an imprint of Skyhorse Publishing, Inc.®, a Delaware corporation.

Visit our website at www.goodbooks.com.

10 9 8 7 6 5 4 3 2 1

Library of Congress Cataloging-in-Publication Data is available on file.

Cover design by Mona Lin
Cover photos by Bonnie Matthews and Clare Barboza

Print ISBN: 978-1-68099-602-9
Ebook ISBN: 978-1-68099-638-8

Printed in China

Table of Contents

About Welcome Home Healthy Cookbook!

We've pulled together the *best* 150 healthy recipes from stovetop, to oven, to slow cooker, and compiled them into one incredible cookbook for you! Whether you're looking for low-fat, low-carb, low-sugar, low-sodium, low-calorie, vegetarian, or even gluten-free recipes, we've got you covered with this wide assortment of recipes.

As you begin journeying through this book, I always suggest reading from cover to cover. I can't tell you the good recipes I've passed on in the past by not following this advice. Don't become overwhelmed. Bookmark or dog-ear the pages of the recipes that interest you the most as you go through. Then, when you've looked at everything, go back to those marked pages and pick two or three to start with. You may even consider choosing a recipe or two you already have the ingredients on hand for. If not, start that grocery list and get to your local store and grab only what you need.

Once you've made a couple recipes from this book, I challenge you to make one that seems "hard" for you! You may just surprise yourself! Putting healthy food on your table has never been easier!

A Note on Nutrition Information

When a recipe lists a range of servings (eg, "makes 6-8 servings"), the highest number of servings is used to calculate nutrition information, resulting in the lowest number of calories, grams of fat, etc. per serving.

Appetizers and Snacks

Hummus from Scratch

Melanie Thrower, McPherson, KS
Makes 24 servings; about 2 Tbsp./ serving

Prep. Time: 10 minutes & *Soaking Time: 8 hours, or overnight* & *Cooking Time: 1½ hours*

16-oz. bag dried chickpeas (garbanzo beans)
⅔ cup lemon juice
3 cloves garlic
⅔ cup peanut butter or tahini (sesame seed paste)
½ cup chopped cilantro
2–3 Tbsp. ground cumin
1 Tbsp. olive oil

1. Place chickpeas in large stockpot. Cover with water. Let stand overnight.

2. In the morning, discard soaking water.

3. Cover with fresh water.

4. Cover and cook 1–1½ hours over low-medium heat, or until tender.

5. Drain off any liquid. Pour beans into food processor.

6. Add all other ingredients, except olive oil, to processor.

7. Blend until smooth. Add additional lemon juice and cumin to suit your taste.

8. Place hummus in serving dish. Drizzle with olive oil.

9. Serve as a dip with cut-up fresh vegetables, baked chips, or pita bread. Or use as a spread on a sandwich with vegetables.

Tip:
You can freeze the hummus and use it up to a week later.

Per Serving
Calories 133, Kilojoules 556, Protein 6 g,
Carbohydrates 16 g, Total Fat 5 g, Saturated Fat 0.7 g,
Monounsaturated Fat 2.3 g, Polyunsaturated Fat 2 g,
Cholesterol 0 mg, Sodium 39 mg, Fiber 6 g

Guacamole

Joyce Shackelford, Green Bay, WI
Makes 5 cups; ½ cup/serving

Prep. Time: 15 minutes

3 avocados, peeled
¼ cup onion minced
¾ tsp. garlic powder
½ tsp. chili powder
2 Tbsp. lemon juice
1 large ripe tomato, chopped

1. Cut avocados in half and remove seed. With spoon scoop out insides and put in medium bowl. Add onion, garlic and chili powders, and lemon juice.

2. With a masher, squash avocados until creamy.

3. Chop tomato and fold in, mixing everything together well.

4. Serve as a dip, sandwich filling, or garnish.

Serving Suggestion:

This goes great with baked tortilla chips, on a salad, or on some whole-grain toast.

Per Serving

Calories 73, Kilojoules 305, Protein 1 g,
Carbohydrates 5 g, Total Fat 5 g, Saturated Fat 0.5 g,
Monounsaturated Fat 4 g, Polyunsaturated Fat 0.5 g,
Cholesterol 0 mg, Sodium 5 mg, Fiber 3 g

Seven Layer Dip

SLOW COOKER

Hope Comerford, Clinton Township, MI
Makes 10–15 servings

Prep. Time: 20 minutes ⚬ Cooking Time: 2 hours ⚬ Ideal slow cooker size: 6-qt.

1 lb. lean ground turkey
2½ tsp. chili powder, divided
½ tsp. kosher salt
⅛ tsp. pepper
15-oz. can fat-free refried beans
4-oz. can diced green chilies
1 cup non-fat Greek yogurt
1 cup salsa
1 cup shredded Mexican blend cheese
2-oz. can sliced black olives
2 green onions, sliced

1. Brown the ground turkey with 1 tsp. chili powder, salt, and pepper.

2. Meanwhile spray the crock with non-stick spray.

3. Mix together 1 tsp. chili powder with the refried beans, then spread them into a layer at the bottom of the crock.

4. Next add a layer of the diced green chilies.

5. Spread the ground turkey over the top of the green chilies.

6. Mix together the remaining ½ tsp. chili powder with the Greek yogurt, and then spread this over the ground turkey in the crock.

7. Next, spread the salsa over the top.

8. Last, sprinkle the cheese into a layer on top and end with the black olives.

9. Cover and cook on low for 2 hours. Sprinkle the green onions on top before serving.

Serving Suggestion:
This would be good with some baked tortilla chips, or sliced bell peppers to dip.

Per Serving

Calories 135, Kilojoules 525, Protein 12 g, Carbohydrates 11 g, Total Fat 6 g, Saturated Fat 3 g, Monounsaturated Fat 1 g, Polyunsaturated Fat 0.7 g, Cholesterol 32 mg, Sodium 420 mg, Fiber 2 g

Lightened-Up Spinach Artichoke Dip

SLOW COOKER

Hope Comerford, Clinton Township, MI
Makes 6–8 servings

Prep. Time: 10 minutes & Cooking Time: 3–4 hours & Ideal slow cooker size: 3- or 4-qt.

10-oz. bag fresh baby spinach, roughly chopped

13.75-oz. can quartered artichoke hearts, drained and chopped

8-oz. brick reduced-fat cream cheese

1 cup non-fat plain Greek yogurt

1 cup shredded mozzarella cheese

½ cup grated Parmesan cheese

½ cup chopped onion

¼ cup chopped green onion

1. Spray your crock with non-stick spray.

2. Combine all ingredients in crock, making sure everything is well-mixed.

3. Cover and cook on low for 3–4 hours, or until the cheese is melted and the dip is heated all the way through.

Serving suggestion:

Serve with brown rice crackers, gluten-free pita bread, or fresh carrot sticks.

Per Serving
Calories 200, Kilojoules 1076, Protein 13 g,
Carbohydrates 7g, Total Fat 12 g, Saturated Fat 8.5 g,
Monounsaturated Fat 4g, Polyunsaturated Fat 0.7 g,
Cholesterol 51 mg, Sodium 633 mg, Fiber 4 g

Fresh Salsa

Barbara Kuhns, Millersburg, OH
Makes 3 cups; ½ cup/serving

Prep. Time: 20 minutes

3 tomatoes
½ cup green sweet bell peppers
¼ cup onions, chopped
1 tsp. garlic powder
1 tsp. cumin
¼ tsp. ground red pepper
2 tsp. vinegar
1 tsp. olive oil
2 tsp. lemon juice

1. Chop vegetables.

2. Add remaining ingredients and mix well.

3. Serve.

Serving suggestion:
This goes great with baked tortilla chips, or used as dressing on your salad.

Per Serving
Calories 26, Kilojoules 109, Protein 1 g,
Carbohydrates 4 g, Total Fat 1 g, Saturated Fat 0.1 g,
Monounsaturated Fat 0.6 g, Polyunsaturated Fat 0.3 g,
Cholesterol 0 mg, Sodium 5 mg, Fiber 1 g

Black Bean Salsa

Barbara Tenney, Delta, PA
Makes 7½ cups; ⅓ cup/serving

Prep. Time: 15 minutes

2 15-oz. cans black beans, rinsed and drained

2 cups fresh corn, cooked or 16-oz. can whole-kernel corn, rinsed and drained

4 Roma/plum tomatoes, seeded and chopped

1 large avocado, peeled and chopped

½ cup red onion, finely chopped

¼ cup chopped fresh cilantro, according to your taste preference

3 Tbsp. lime juice

1 Tbsp. olive oil

1 Tbsp. red wine vinegar

½ tsp. freshly ground pepper

1. Combine all ingredients in large bowl.
2. Cover and chill.

Serving suggestion:

Serve with baked tortilla chips.

Per Serving

Calories 56, Kilojoules 234, Protein 2 g,
Carbohydrates 9 g, Total Fat 1.7 g, Saturated Fat 0.2 g,
Monounsaturated Fat 1 g, Polyunsaturated Fat 0.5 g,
Cholesterol 0 mg, Sodium 77 mg, Fiber 3 g

Fruit Salsa

Maryann Markano, Wilmington, DE
Makes 4 servings; ⅓ cup/serving

Prep. Time: 15 minutes ⚹ *Marinating Time: 20 minutes*

¾ cup chopped strawberries

⅓ cup chopped blueberries

2 Tbsp. chopped green bell sweet
pepper

2 Tbsp. chopped carrot

1 Tbsp. chopped onion

2 tsp. cider vinegar

1 tsp. minced jalapeño pepper*

1. Combine all ingredients in small bowl.

2. Let stand 20 minutes to allow flavors to blend.

* Note:

Wear gloves and wash hands
after chopping jalapeño.

Per Serving

Calories 19, Kilojoules 79, Protein trace,
Carbohydrates 5 g, Total Fat trace, Saturated Fat trace,
Monounsaturated Fat trace, Polyunsaturated Fat trace,
Cholesterol 0 mg, Sodium 3 mg, Fiber 1 g

Fat-Free Strawberry Yogurt Dip

Katrina Eberly, Stevens, PA
Makes 14 servings; approximately ¼ cup/serving

Prep. Time: 15 minutes

1 ½ cups fresh, or frozen, whole strawberries

8 oz. fat-free strawberry yogurt, sweetened with low-calorie sweetener

1 cup fat-free whipped topping

Assorted fruit, or angel food cake

1. In a bowl, mash berries.

2. Add yogurt and mix well.

3. Fold in whipped topping.

4. Serve with fruit or cake.

Per Serving
Calories 32, Kilojoules 134, Protein 1 g,
Carbohydrates 7 g, Total Fat 0.2 g, Saturated Fat 0.1 g,
Monounsaturated Fat 0.07 g, Polyunsaturated Fat 0.03 g,
Cholesterol 1 mg, Sodium 13 mg, Fiber 0.3 g

Munchie Mix

Dena Tompkins, Huntersville, NC
Makes 6½ cups; ¼ cup/serving

Prep. Time: 10 minutes

I cup roasted unsalted soy nuts

1 ½ cups shelled walnuts, whole or halved

I cup roasted, unsalted sunflower kernels

I cup multigrain pretzel sticks, broken in half

½ cup banana chips

½ cup dried blueberries

½ cup dried cherries

1. Mix all ingredients in large mixing bowl and serve.

Tips:

1. You can substitute pumpernickel sticks for the multigrain sticks to change the flavor.

2. You can make this ahead of time and then divide it into plastic individual snack-bag servings. These will be ready to grab and go. Prepared servings discourage overeating.

Per Serving

Calories 136, Kilojoules 569, Protein 4 g, Carbohydrates 12 g, Total Fat 8 g, Saturated Fat 1.5 g, Monounsaturated Fat 1.5 g, Polyunsaturated Fat 5 g, Cholesterol 0 mg, Sodium 48 mg, Fiber 3 g

Gluten-Free Chex Mix

SLOW COOKER

Hope Comerford, Clinton Township, MI
Makes 12 servings

Prep. Time: 8 minutes ⚜ *Cooking Time: 3 hours* ⚜ *Cooling Time: 1 hour* ⚜ *Ideal slow cooker size: 6- or 7-qt.*

3 cups gluten-free Rice Chex

3 cups gluten-free Corn Chex

3 cups gluten-free Cheerios

1 cup unsalted peanuts

⅓ cup coconut oil, melted

4 tsp. gluten-free Worcestershire sauce

1 tsp. sea salt

1 tsp. garlic powder

1 tsp. onion powder

1. Spray the crock with non-stick spray.

2. Place the Rice Chex, Corn Chex, Cheerios, and peanuts in the crock.

3. In a small bowl, whisk together the coconut oil, Worcestershire, sea salt, garlic powder, and onion powder. Pour this over the cereal in the crock and gently mix it with a rubber spatula until all cereal and peanuts are evenly coated.

4. Place a paper towel or thin dishcloth under the lid and cook on low for 3 hours, stirring once at the end of the first hour, once at the end of the second hour, and twice the last hour.

5. Spread the mixture onto parchment paper-lined baking sheets and let them cool for 1 hour.

6. Serve or keep in a sealed container at room temperature for up to 3 weeks.

Per Serving

Calories 210, Kilojoules 869, Protein 5 g,
Carbohydrates 21 g, Total Fat 13 g, Saturated Fat 6 g,
Monounsaturated Fat 4 g, Polyunsaturated Fat 1.4 g,
Cholesterol 0 mg, Sodium 350 mg, Fiber 0 g

Lettuce Wraps

SLOW COOKER

Hope Comerford, Clinton Township, MI
Makes About 12 wraps

Prep. Time: 15 minutes & Cooking Time: 2–3 hours & Ideal slow cooker size: 5- or 7-qt.

2 lb. ground chicken, browned

4 cloves garlic, minced

½ cup minced sweet yellow onion

4 Tbsp. gluten-free soy sauce or Bragg's liquid aminos

1 Tbsp. natural crunchy peanut butter

1 tsp. rice wine vinegar

1 tsp. sesame oil

¼ tsp. kosher salt

¼ tsp. red pepper flakes

¼ tsp. black pepper

8-oz. can sliced water chestnuts, drained, rinsed, chopped

3 green onions, sliced

12 good-sized pieces of iceberg lettuce, rinsed and patted dry

1. In the crock, combine the ground chicken, garlic, yellow onion, soy sauce or liquid aminos, peanut butter, vinegar, sesame oil, salt, red pepper flakes, and black pepper.

2. Cover and cook on low for 2–3 hours.

3. Add in the water chestnuts and green onions. Cover and cook for an additional 10–15 minutes.

4. Serve a good spoonful on each piece of iceberg lettuce.

Serving suggestion:

Garnish with diced red bell pepper and diced green onion.

Per Serving
Calories 135, Kilojoules 600, Protein 14.5 g,
Carbohydrates 3.5 g, Total Fat 7 g, Saturated Fat 3 g,
Monounsaturated Fat 3 g, Polyunsaturated Fat 1.3 g,
Cholesterol 65 mg, Sodium 430 mg, Fiber 1 g

Quesadilla Roll-Ups

Betty Moore, Plano, IL
Makes 16 servings; 2 pieces/serving

Prep. Time: 15 minutes ⚶ *Baking Time: 13–18 minutes*

4-oz. can diced green chili peppers, drained

½ small onion, diced

¼ tsp. ground cumin

8 10" fat-free flour tortillas

2 cups (8 oz.) shredded reduced-fat Monterey Jack cheese

1. In bowl combine peppers, onion, and cumin.

2. Sprinkle each tortilla with cheese using ¼ cup cheese on each.

3. Divide pepper mixture between tortillas, spreading it over cheese.

4. Roll up each tortilla and put in greased 9 × 13 baking pan. Cover pan with foil. Bake at 350° for 10–15 minutes, or until cheese melts.

5. Remove foil. Turn oven to broil.

6. Broil 4″ from heat for 1½ minutes per side, or until lightly browned.

7. Cut each tortilla into 4 pieces.

8. Serve with your favorite salsa for dipping.

Per Serving

Calories 103, Kilojoules 431, Protein 6 g,
Carbohydrates 16 g, Total Fat 3 g, Saturated Fat 1.5 g,
Monounsaturated Fat 0.5 g, Polyunsaturated Fat 1 g,
Cholesterol 10 mg, Sodium 200 mg, Fiber 6 g

Mini Eggplant Pizzas

Maryann Markano, Wilmington, DE
Makes 4 servings

Prep. Time: 20 minutes ⚜ *Cooking/Baking Time: 11–13 minutes*

1 eggplant, 3" diameter
1 ½ tsp. fresh chopped oregano
½ tsp. fresh chopped basil
1 clove garlic, crushed
1 Tbsp. olive oil
⅛ tsp. black pepper
1 large ripe tomato, cut into 4 slices
¼ cup low-sodium, low-fat pizza sauce
½ cup shredded reduced-fat
mozzarella cheese

1. Preheat oven to 425°.

2. Peel eggplant and cut into 4 ½"-thick slices.

3. Combine herbs and set aside.

4. Brush both sides of eggplant with oil and season with pepper.

5. Arrange on baking sheet and bake until browned, about 8 minutes. Turn once during baking to brown both sides.

6. Place a tomato slice on each eggplant slice and sprinkle with spice mixture. Drizzle each slice with 1 Tbsp. pizza sauce.

7. Top with cheese and bake until cheese melts, about 3–5 minutes. Serve hot.

Per Serving

Calories 128, Kilojoules 536, Protein 6 g,
Carbohydrates 13 g, Total Fat 5 g, Saturated Fat 1.5 g,
Monounsaturated Fat 3 g, Polyunsaturated Fat 0.5 g,
Cholesterol 5 mg, Sodium 133 mg, Fiber 5 g

Avocado Egg Salad

Melanie Mohler, Ephrata, PA
Makes 4 servings

Prep. Time: 10 minutes

4 eggs, hard-cooked and chopped
(reserve 2 yolks for another use)
1 clove garlic, minced
1 large avocado, chopped
Pepper to taste
2 Tbsp. fresh lemon juice

1. In a serving bowl, combine eggs, garlic and avocado.

2. Sprinkle with pepper and lemon juice. Stir gently.

3. Use as topping for crackers or as sandwich filling. Eat immediately or store in fridge.

Per Serving

Calories 101, Kilojoules 423, Protein 5 g,
Carbohydrates 4 g, Total Fat 7 g, Saturated Fat 1.5 g,
Monounsaturated Fat 4.5 g, Polyunsaturated Fat 1 g,
Cholesterol 104 mg, Sodium 61 mg, Fiber 2.5 g

Breakfast and Brunches

Berry-Topped Wheat Pancakes

Anne Nolt, Thompsontown, PA
Makes 6 servings

Prep. Time: 10 minutes  *Cooking Time: 15–20 minutes*

I cup whole wheat pastry flour

½ cup wheat germ

I Tbsp. sugar

2 tsp. baking powder

¼ tsp. baking soda

¾ cup orange juice

¾ cup fat-free plain yogurt

2 Tbsp. canola oil

Egg substitute equivalent to I large egg,
or 2 egg whites

2 cups blueberries

Blueberry Sauce

¼ cup sugar

2 Tbsp. cornstarch

I cup water

4 cups blueberries

1. In medium bowl, combine dry ingredients. Mix well.

2. In small bowl, combine orange juice, yogurt, oil, and egg. Blend well.

3. Add liquid ingredients to dry ingredients.

4. Add 2 cups blueberries.

5. Stir everything together gently, just until dry ingredients are moistened.

6. Pour batter by ¼ cup-fuls onto hot, lightly greased griddle or into large skillet.

7. Turn when bubbles form on top.

8. Cook until second side is golden brown.

9. Serve with Blueberry Sauce.

1. In medium saucepan combine sugar and cornstarch. Gradually stir in water.

2. Add blueberries.

3. Bring to a boil over medium heat.

4. Boil 2 minutes, stirring constantly.

5. Remove from heat. Serve with pancakes.

Per Serving

Calories 300, Kilojoules 1255,

Protein 8 g,

Carbohydrates 58 g, Total Fat 5 g,

Saturated Fat 0.5 g,

Monounsaturated Fat 3 g,

Polyunsaturated Fat 1.5 g,

Cholesterol 0 mg, Sodium 175 mg,

Fiber 7 g

Pumpkin Spice Pancakes

Christie Detamore-Hunsberger, Harrisonburg, VA
Makes 12 pancakes, 2 pancakes per serving

Prep. Time: 10 minutes   Cooking Time: 15–20 minutes

1 cup whole wheat pastry flour
1 tsp. baking powder
½ tsp. baking soda
½ tsp. cinnamon
½ tsp. ground ginger
½ tsp. nutmeg
¾ cup pumpkin
¾ cup skim milk
½ cup plain non-fat yogurt
2 Tbsp. oil
1 large egg, beaten

1. In a mixing bowl, combine 6 dry ingredients.

2. Stir in 5 wet ingredients.

3. When well combined, drop by ¼ cupfuls onto griddle or into skillet.

4. Cook until bubbles form on top.

5. Flip. Cook until second side is golden brown.

Tip:

These pancakes turn into a party if you serve them with ginger butter (please note that the butter ingredients are not included in the recipe's nutritional analyses): ¼ cup (half a stick) softened butter, 1 tsp. candied or fresh ginger, 1 lb. powdered sugar. Stir together in a large bowl until smooth. (Add more ground ginger to the pancake batter itself for a more intense taste.)

Per Serving

Calories 146, Kilojoules 611, Protein 6 g, Carbohydrates 20 g, Total Fat 5 g, Saturated Fat 0.5 g, Monounsaturated Fat 3 g, Polyunsaturated Fat 1.5 g, Cholesterol 1 mg, Sodium 195 mg, Fiber 4 g

Multigrain Pancakes

Deborah Heatwole, Waynesboro, GA
Makes 6 servings

Prep. Time: 5–10 minutes ⚜ *Cooking Time: 10–15 minutes*

1 cup whole wheat pastry flour

½ cup all-purpose flour

¼ cup cornmeal

¼ cup buckwheat flour

2 tsp. baking powder

¼ tsp. baking soda

egg substitute equivalent to 2 eggs, or
4 egg whites

1 Tbsp. canola oil

2 cups skim milk

1. In a good-sized bowl, mix together dry ingredients thoroughly.

2. Add egg substitute or whites, oil, and milk. Stir well to combine.

3. Cook by ¼ cupfuls on a non-stick or cast-iron skillet sprayed with non-stick cooking spray.

4. When bubbles begin to form on pancakes, flip and brown other side.

Serving suggestion:

Serve with maple syrup, honey, or your choice of toppings.

Per Serving
Calories 195, Kilojoules 816, Protein 9 g,
Carbohydrates 34 g, Total Fat 3 g, Saturated Fat 0.2 g,
Monounsaturated Fat 1.5 g, Polyunsaturated Fat 1.3 g,
Cholesterol 1.6 mg, Sodium 200 mg, Fiber 3 g

Oatmeal Waffles

Deborah Heatwole, Waynesboro, GA
Makes 6 servings

Prep. Time: 5–10 minutes   Cooking Time: 3–5 minutes

1 cup whole wheat pastry flour
⅔ cup uncooked rolled, or quick, oats
⅓ cup cornmeal
2 tsp. baking powder
¼ tsp. baking soda
2 cups skim milk
1 Tbsp. canola oil
Egg substitute equivalent to 2 eggs, or 4 egg whites, beaten

1. Combine dry ingredients in mixing bowl.

2. Stir in milk, oil, and beaten egg substitute or whites.

3. When batter is well blended, cook in waffle iron according to appliance instructions.

Serving Suggestion:

If you wish, serve with maple syrup, honey, or blueberry preserves (not included in analyses).

Per Serving
Calories 192, Kilojoules 803, Protein 9 g,
Carbohydrates 33 g, Total Fat 3 g, Saturated Fat 0.3 g,
Monounsaturated Fat 1.7 g, Polyunsaturated Fat 1 g,
Cholesterol 1.6 mg, Sodium 200 mg, Fiber 3 g

Baked Blueberry French Toast

Carol Eberly, Harrisonburg, VA
Makes 9 servings

Prep. Time: 15 minutes ❧ *Chilling Time: 8 hours, or overnight* ❧ *Cooking Time: 20 minutes*

12" long French, or sourdough, baguette

4 egg whites

1 cup fat-free soy milk

¼ tsp. nutmeg

1 tsp. vanilla extract

4 Tbsp. brown sugar, divided

¾ cup blueberries, coarsely chopped

1 Tbsp. canola oil

¼ cup chopped pecans, toasted, optional (not included in analyses)

1. Spray 9" square baking dish with cooking spray.

2. Cut 10 1"-thick slices from baguette. Arrange in baking dish.

3. In a large bowl, whisk egg whites until frothy.

4. Then whisk in milk, nutmeg, vanilla, and 2 tablespoons brown sugar.

5. Pour evenly over bread, turning slices to coat evenly.

6. Cover pan. Chill at least 8 hours or overnight, until liquid is absorbed by bread.

7. Preheat oven to 400°.

8. Drop blueberries evenly over bread.

9. In a small bowl, stir together 2 tablespoons brown sugar and oil, and pecans if you wish. Spoon evenly over bread.

10. Bake, uncovered, about 20 minutes, until liquid from blueberries is bubbling.

Serving Suggestion:

Serve with pure maple syrup (not included in analyses) if you wish.

Per Serving

Calories 146, Kilojoules 611, Protein 5 g, Carbohydrates 25 g, Total Fat 3 g, Saturated Fat 0.5 g, Monounsaturated Fat 1.5 g, Polyunsaturated Fat 1 g, Cholesterol 0 mg, Sodium 259 mg, Fiber 1

Banana Oat Breakfast Cookies

Mary Ann Lefever, Lancaster, PA
Makes 12 cookies; 1 cookie/serving

Prep. Time: 15 minutes   ❧   *Baking Time: 14–15 minutes, per baking sheet*

I large banana, mashed (about ½ cup)

½ cup chunky natural (unsalted and unsweetened) peanut butter, or regular chunky peanut butter

½ cup honey

I tsp. vanilla extract

I cup uncooked rolled oats

½ cup whole wheat pastry flour

¼ cup non-fat dry milk powder

2 tsp. ground cinnamon

¼ tsp. baking soda

I cup dried cranberries, or raisins

1. Preheat oven to 350°. Lightly coat two baking sheets with non-stick cooking spray. Set aside.

2. In large bowl, stir together banana, peanut butter, honey, and vanilla.

3. In a small bowl, combine oats, flour, milk powder, cinnamon, and baking soda.

4. Stir oat mixture into banana mixture until combined.

5. Stir in dried cranberries.

6. Using a ¼-cup measure, drop dough into mounds 3″ apart on prepared baking sheets.

7. With a thick spatula dipped in water, flatten and spread each dough mound into a 2¾″-round, about ½″ thick.

8. Bake, one sheet at a time, 14–16 minutes, or until cookies are lightly browned.

9. Transfer cookies to wire racks to cool completely.

Tip:

Store in airtight container or re-sealable plastic bag for up to three days, or freeze for up to two months. Thaw before serving.

Per Serving

Calories 203, Kilojoules 849, Protein 5 g, Carbohydrates 35 g, Total Fat 5 g, Saturated Fat 1 g, Monounsaturated Fat 2.5 g, Polyunsaturated Fat 1.5 g, Cholesterol 0.3 mg, Sodium 92 mg, Fiber 3 g

Baked Oatmeal

Lovina Baer, Conrath, WI
Edwina Stoltzfus, Narvon, PA
Makes 8 servings

Prep. Time: 10 minutes   ❧   *Baking Time: 30 minutes*

1 Tbsp. canola oil

½ cup unsweetened applesauce

⅓ cup brown sugar

Egg substitute equivalent to 2 eggs, or 4 egg whites

3 cups uncooked rolled oats

2 tsp. baking powder

1 tsp. cinnamon

1 cup skim milk

1. In a good-sized bowl, stir together oil, applesauce, sugar, and eggs.

2. Add dry ingredients and milk. Mix well.

3. Spray 9 × 13 baking pan generously with non-stick cooking spray. Spoon oatmeal mixture into pan.

4. Bake uncovered at 350° for 30 minutes.

Tip:

You can mix this in the evening and refrigerate it overnight. Just pop it in the oven first thing when you get up.

Per Serving

Calories 204, Kilojoules 854, Protein 8 g,
Carbohydrates 34 g, Total Fat 4 g, Saturated Fat 0.7 g,
Monounsaturated Fat 1.9 g, Polyunsaturated Fat 1.4 g,
Cholesterol 0.5 mg, Sodium 105 mg, Fiber 4 g

Apple Oatmeal

SLOW COOKER

Frances B. Musser, Newmanstown, PA
Makes 5 servings

Prep. Time: 20 minutes ⚜ *Cooking Time: 3–5 hours* ⚜ *Ideal slow cooker size: 3-qt.*

2 cups fat-free milk
1 cup water
1 Tbsp. honey
1 Tbsp. coconut oil
¼ tsp. kosher salt
½ tsp. cinnamon
1 cup gluten-free steel-cut oats
1 cup chopped apples
½ cup chopped walnuts
1 Tbsp. turbinado sugar

1. Grease the inside of the slow cooker crock.

2. Add all ingredients to crock and mix.

3. Cover. Cook on low 3–5 hours.

Per Serving

Calories 337, Kilojoules 1411, Protein 11 g,
Carbohydrates 46 g, Total Fat 13 g, Saturated Fat 3 g,
Monounsaturated Fat 1 g, Polyunsaturated Fat 5.6 g,
Cholesterol 2 mg, Sodium 140 mg, Fiber 6 g

European Breakfast Muesli

Willard Roth, Elkhart, IN
Makes 5 servings; approximately ⅔ cup/serving

Prep. Time: 10 minutes ♣ Chilling Time: 2–8 hours

1 cup whole grain quick oats, uncooked

6 oz. fat-free vanilla yogurt, sweetened with low-calorie sweetener

1 cup skim milk

¼ cup honey

⅓ cup ground flaxseed

½ cup dried cherries, or dried cranberries

1 cup fresh, or frozen, blueberries

5 tsp. sliced almonds

1. Combine all ingredients except blueberries and almonds in bowl. Stir well.

2. Cover and refrigerate at least two hours (overnight is preferable).

3. Serve as is, first dividing blueberries among the 5 servings. Then top each serving with 1 tsp. sliced almonds.

Tip:

Leftover portion may be refrigerated for several days.

Per Serving
Calories 293, Kilojoules 1226, Protein 8 g,
Carbohydrates 55 g, Total Fat 5 g, Saturated Fat 0.5 g,
Monounsaturated Fat 1.5 g, Polyunsaturated Fat 3 g,
Cholesterol 1 mg, Sodium 51 mg, Fiber 7 g

Blueberry and Oatmeal Breakfast Cake

Jean Butzer, Batavia, NY
Makes 8 servings

Prep. Time: 15 minutes   ❧   Baking Time: 25 minutes

1½ cups whole wheat pastry flour

¾ cup uncooked rolled oats

⅓ cup sugar

2 tsp. baking powder

¼ tsp. cinnamon, optional

¾ cup skim milk

2 Tbsp. canola oil

2 Tbsp. mashed banana, or unsweetened applesauce

Egg substitute equivalent to 1 egg, or 2 egg whites

1 cup blueberries, fresh or frozen

1. Preheat oven to 400°. Spray 8″ round baking pan with cooking spray.

2. Combine flour, oats, sugar, baking powder, and cinnamon if you wish, in medium-sized mixing bowl.

3. In 2-cup measure, mix milk, oil, mashed banana or applesauce, and egg.

4. Add wet ingredients to flour mixture. Stir until just moistened.

5. Gently fold in blueberries.

6. Spoon into baking pan.

7. Bake, uncovered, 20–25 minutes, or until tester inserted in center of cake comes out clean.

Per Serving

Calories 211, Kilojoules 883, Protein 9 g,
Carbohydrates 33 g, Total Fat 5 g, Saturated Fat 0.5 g,
Monounsaturated Fat 2.5 g, Polyunsaturated Fat 2 g,
Cholesterol 1 mg, Sodium 125 mg, Fiber 4 g

Granola in the Slow Cooker

SLOW COOKER

Earnie Zimmerman, Mechanicsburg, PA
Makes 10–12 servings

Prep. Time: 10 minutes ♣ Cooking Time: 3–8 hours ♣ Ideal slow cooker size: 6-qt.

5 cups gluten-free rolled oats

1 Tbsp. flaxseeds

¼ cup slivered almonds

¼ cup chopped pecans or walnuts

¼ cup unsweetened shredded coconut

¼ cup maple syrup or honey

¼ cup melted coconut oil

½ cup dried fruit

1. Spray slow cooker crock with cooking spray. In slow cooker, mix together oats, flaxseeds, almonds, pecans or walnuts, and coconut.

2. Separately, combine maple syrup or honey and coconut oil. Pour over dry ingredients in cooker and toss well.

3. Place lid on slow cooker with a wooden spoon handle or chopstick venting one end of the lid.

4. Cook on high for 3–4 hours, stirring every 30 minutes, or cook on low for 8 hours, stirring every hour. You may need to stir more often or cook for less time, depending on how hot your cooker cooks.

5. When granola smells good and toasty, pour it out onto a baking sheet to cool.

6. Add dried fruit to cooled granola and store in airtight container.

Per Serving

Calories 273, Kilojoules 1146, Protein 7 g,
Carbohydrates 37 g, Total Fat 11 g, Saturated Fat 5 g,
Monounsaturated Fat 2 g, Polyunsaturated Fat 1 g,
Cholesterol 0 mg, Sodium 7 mg, Fiber 5 g

Peanut Butter Granola

Yvonne Kauffman Boettger, Harrisonburg, VA
Makes 16 cups; ¼ cup per serving

Prep. Time: 15 minutes   ⚬   *Cooking Time: 37–38 minutes*

I cup honey

½ cup canola, or olive, oil

I cup natural peanut butter, no salt added

½ tsp. salt

I Tbsp. cinnamon

I cup water

12 cups uncooked rolled oats

I cup chopped pecans

I cup cornmeal

I cup ground flaxseed

I cup wheat germ

1. Combine first 6 ingredients in microwave-safe bowl. Microwave on high 2–3 minutes.

2. Stir until peanut butter is melted.

3. Combine remaining ingredients in a large mixing bowl.

4. Add liquids and mix well.

5. Divide between two greased 9 × 13 baking pans.

6. Bake, uncovered, at 325° for 20 minutes.

7. Stir and bake, uncovered, another 15 minutes.

8. When completely cool, break up granola and store in containers with tight-fitting lids. Store in fridge or freezer.

Per Serving

Calories 151, Kilojoules 632, Protein 4 g, Carbohydrates 22 g, Total Fat 5 g, Saturated Fat 1 g, Monounsaturated Fat 2.5 g, Polyunsaturated Fat 1.5 g, Cholesterol 0 mg, Sodium 20 mg, Fiber 3 g

Homemade Turkey Sausage

Becky Frey, Lebanon, PA
Makes 6 servings

Prep. Time: 10 minutes ⚓ Broiling Time: 10–15 minutes

¾ lb. extra-lean skinless turkey, ground
¼ tsp. pepper
¼ tsp. dried basil
¼ tsp. dried sage
¼ tsp. dried oregano
1 egg white
⅛ tsp. allspice
⅛ tsp. nutmeg
⅛ tsp. garlic powder
⅛ tsp. chili powder
⅛ tsp. Tabasco sauce, optional
2 Tbsp. water

1. Mix all ingredients together in a large bowl.

2. Shape into 6 patties. Place on baking sheet.

3. Broil 2–3" from heat 5–7 minutes.

4. Flip burgers over. Broil 5–7 more minutes.

Tips:

1. This turkey sausage can be shaped into meatballs and used with spaghetti or another favorite sauce.

2. I often brown this sausage and use it in any casserole in which I want a sausage flavor, but without the extra fat or salt of commercially made sausage.

Per Serving
Calories 64, Kilojoules 268, Protein 14 g,
Carbohydrates trace, Total Fat 1 g, Saturated Fat 0.2 g,
Monounsaturated Fat 0.7 g, Polyunsaturated Fat 0.1 g,
Cholesterol 22 mg, Sodium 50 mg, Fiber trace

Slow Cooker Yogurt

SLOW COOKER

Becky Fixel, Grosse Pointe Farms, MI
Makes 12–14 servings

Prep. Time: 2 minutes   ♣   Cooking Time: 12–14 hours   ♣   Ideal slow cooker size: 6-qt.

1 gallon whole milk
5.3 oz. Greek yogurt with cultures

1. Empty the gallon of whole milk into your slow cooker and put it on high heat for 2–4 hours. Length of time depends on your model, but the milk needs to heat to just below boiling point, about 180–200°.

2. Turn off your slow cooker and let your milk cool down to 110–115°. Again, this will take 2–4 hours. Set your starter Greek yogurt out so it can reach room temperature during this step.

3. In a small bowl, add about 1 cup of the warm milk and the Greek yogurt and mix together. Pour the mixture into the milk in the slow cooker and mix it in by stirring back and forth. Replace the lid of your slow cooker and wrap the whole thing in a towel. Let sit for 12–14 hours, or in other words, go to bed.

4. After 12 hours check on your glorious yogurt!

5. Line a colander with cheesecloth and place in bowl. Scoop your yogurt inside and let it sit for at least 4 hours. This will help separate the extra whey from the yogurt and thicken your final yogurt.

Tip:

"My yogurt didn't all fit in one colander, but thankfully I had a second one to use. You can wait until the yogurt sinks down and there is more space in the colander if you only have one. Spoon finished yogurt into jars or containers and place in the fridge. After your yogurt is done, you're going to have leftover whey. Put it in a jar and pop it in the fridge. Use it to replace stock in recipes, water your plants, or to make cheese. It's amazing what you can do with it!"

—Becky Fixel

Per Serving

Calories 180, Kilojoules 755, Protein 10 g, Carbohydrates 14 g, Total Fat 10 g, Saturated Fat 5 g, Monounsaturated Fat 2 g, Polyunsaturated Fat 0.6 g, Cholesterol 29 mg, Sodium 124 mg, Fiber 0 g

Italian Frittata

SLOW COOKER

Hope Comerford, Clinton Township, MI
Makes 6 servings

Prep. Time: 10 minutes & Cooking Time: 3–4 hours & Ideal slow cooker size: 5- or 6-qt.

10 eggs
1 Tbsp. chopped fresh basil
1 Tbsp. chopped fresh mint
1 Tbsp. chopped fresh sage
1 Tbsp. chopped fresh oregano
½ tsp. sea salt
⅛ tsp. pepper
1 Tbsp. grated Parmesan cheese
¼ cup diced prosciutto
½ cup chopped onion

1. Spray your crock with non-stick spray.

2. In a bowl, mix together the eggs, basil, mint, sage, oregano, sea salt, pepper, and Parmesan. Pour this mixture into the crock.

3. Sprinkle the prosciutto and onion evenly over the egg mixture in the crock.

4. Cover and cook on low for 3–4 hours.

Per Serving

Calories 137, Kilojoules 576, Protein 12 g,
Carbohydrates 2 g, Total Fat 9 g, Saturated Fat 3 g,
Monounsaturated Fat 3 g, Polyunsaturated Fat 1.7 g,
Cholesterol 312 mg, Sodium 327 mg, Fiber 0 g

Spinach Mushroom Frittata

JB Miller, Indianapolis, IN
Makes 6 servings

Prep. Time: 20 minutes ⚘ *Cooking/Baking Time: 25–30 minutes*

3 cloves garlic, minced
1 cup onion, chopped
1 tsp. olive oil
½ lb. fresh mushrooms, sliced
½ tsp. dried thyme
10-oz. bag fresh spinach
Egg substitute equivalent to 10 eggs
1 tsp. dried dill, or 1 Tbsp. fresh dill
¼ tsp. black pepper
¼ cup feta cheese

Tips:

1. If the pan is not prepared properly with vegetable spray, the frittata will stick to the bottom.

2. Flipping the frittata onto the serving plate is best done with two people!

Per Serving

Calories 117, Kilojoules 490, Protein 12 g,
Carbohydrates 9 g, Total Fat 3 g,
Saturated Fat 1 g,
Monounsaturated Fat 1.3 g,
Polyunsaturated Fat 0.7 g,
Cholesterol 5 mg, Sodium 300 mg, Fiber 3 g

1. Preheat oven to 350°.

2. In a large 10″ or 12″ non-stick skillet, sauté garlic and onions in 1 teaspoon olive oil for about 5 minutes.

3. Add mushrooms and thyme. Cook an additional 5 minutes. Remove skillet from stove.

4. Place spinach in a separate saucepan. Add 1 Tbsp. water. Cover and cook until just wilted.

5. Drain spinach and let cool in a colander.

6. Squeeze out any liquid. Chop leaves.

7. In a good-sized bowl, beat together egg substitute, dill, and pepper.

8. Stir in spinach, mushroom mixture, and feta cheese.

9. Clean non-stick skillet. Spray liberally with vegetable spray. Return skillet to stove over medium heat.

10. When skillet is hot, pour in egg mixture. Place in oven, uncovered.

11. Check frittata in 10 minutes. Check every 5 minutes thereafter until center of frittata is slightly firm. Do not over-cook.

12. When frittata is done, place a large serving platter over skillet. Flip skillet over so frittata falls onto the plate.

13. Cut into six servings and serve.

Garden Vegetable Quiche

Susan Kasting, Jenks, OK
Makes 9 servings

Prep. Time: 20 minutes ⚮ *Cooking/Baking Time: 40–45 minutes* ⚮ *Standing Time: 10 minutes*

1 ½ cups egg substitute

3 large eggs

⅓ cup skim milk

½ cup whole wheat pastry flour

8 oz. low-sodium fat-free cottage cheese

4 cups sliced zucchini

2 cups diced raw potatoes

3 Tbsp. diced onion

1 cup finely chopped green bell sweet pepper

½ lb. fresh mushrooms, sliced

½ cup chopped parsley

2 tomatoes, thinly sliced

1 cup low-fat cheese of your choice, shredded, divided

1. Preheat oven to 400°.

2. In a large bowl, beat egg substitute and eggs until fluffy.

3. Stir in milk, flour, and cottage cheese.

4. Sauté zucchini, potatoes, onions, peppers, and mushrooms in pan coated with cooking spray for 5 minutes.

5. Stir sautéed vegetable mixture and parsley into egg mixture.

6. When well combined, pour into a 3-quart baking dish, lightly coated with cooking spray.

7. Top with tomato slices and cheese.

8. Bake 35–40 minutes, or until knife inserted in center comes out clean.

9. Allow to stand 10 minutes before slicing.

Per Serving

Calories 195, Kilojoules 816, Protein 17 g,
Carbohydrates 24 g, Total Fat 3 g, Saturated Fat 1.2 g,
Monounsaturated Fat 1 g, Polyunsaturated 0.8 g,
Cholesterol 75 mg, Sodium 210 mg, Fiber 3 g

Breads

14-Grain Bread

Esther Hartzler, Carlsbad, NM
Makes 3 loaves, ½"-thick slice per serving

Prep. Time: 45 minutes ⚬ *Rising Time: 2½– 3 hours* ⚬ *Baking Time: 35–40 minutes*

1 cup dry 9-grain cereal

½ cup unsalted sunflower seeds

2½ Tbsp. sesame seeds

2½ Tbsp. amaranth

1½ Tbsp. yeast

2 cups whole wheat flour, plus more if needed

3 cups warm water

2½ Tbsp. dry millet

2½ Tbsp. flaxseed

⅓ cup canola oil

⅓ cup honey

1 Tbsp. sea salt

¼ cup wheat gluten

1. Place all ingredients in bowl of a strong and sturdy mixer, with a mixer bowl at least 4½ quarts in size. Mix 10 minutes.

2. If needed, add more whole wheat flour until mixture cleans side of bowl.

3. Knead 12 minutes on low speed.

4. Form into 3 loaves. Place each in a 2½ × 4½ × 8½ loaf pan that has been generously sprayed with non-stick cooking spray.

5. Cover pans and place in warm spot. Let rise until double, about 2½–3 hours.

6. Bake at 350° 35–40 minutes.

Tip:

I like to measure the grains and combine them in a ziplock bag, and then freeze them in advance of baking. Keep the whole wheat flour separate, however.

Per Serving

Calories 58, Kilojoules 243, Protein 2 g, Carbohydrates 8 g, Total Fat 2 g, Saturated Fat 0.2 g, Monounsaturated Fat 1 g, Polyunsaturated Fat 0.8 g, Cholesterol trace, Sodium 139 mg, Fiber 1 g

Wholesome Harvest Bread

Kathryn Good, Dayton, VA
Makes 3 loaves, 17 slices/loaf, each sliced ½" thick

Prep. Time: 20–30 minutes ☙ Rising Time: 4–5 hours ☙ Baking Time: 30–35 minutes

½ cup cornmeal
½ cup honey
⅓ cup (5⅓ Tbsp.) butter, or olive oil
I Tbsp. salt
2 cups boiling water
2 pkgs. yeast
½ cup warm water
I tsp. sugar
4 egg whites
I cup rye flour
2 cups whole wheat flour
3 Tbsp. poppy seeds
I cup sunflower seed kernels
4 cups unbleached bread flour

1. In a small bowl, combine cornmeal, honey, butter or olive oil, salt, and boiling water. Let stand until mixture cools to lukewarm.

2. Meanwhile, in a large mixing bowl combine yeast, warm water, and sugar. Stir until yeast and sugar dissolve.

3. Beat egg whites into yeast mixture.

4. When cornmeal mixture is lukewarm, mix into yeast mixture.

5. Stir in rye flour, wheat flour, and seeds.

6. On a lightly floured surface, knead in bread flour until dough is smooth and elastic.

7. Return dough to bowl. Cover and place in a warm spot. Let rise until double, about 2½–3 hours. Form into 3 loaves.

8. Place each in a 2½ × 4½ × 8½ loaf pan that has been generously sprayed with cooking spray.

9. Cover pans and place in a warm spot.

10. Let rise until almost double in size, about 1½–2 hours.

11. Bake at 350° for approximately 30 minutes, or until tops are golden.

Per Serving

Calories 101, Kilojoules 423,
Protein 3 g,
Carbohydrates 17 g, Total Fat 3 g,
Saturated Fat 0.5 g,
Monounsaturated Fat 1.5 g,
Polyunsaturated Fat 1 g,
Cholesterol 0 mg, Sodium 142 mg,
Fiber 1.5 g

The Best Honey Whole Wheat Bread

Pamela Metzler, Gilman, WI

Makes 4 loaves of bread, 17 slices/loaf, each ½" thick

Prep. Time: 20–30 minutes & Rising Time: 3–4 hours & Baking Time: 25 minutes

1 cup dry rolled oats

3 cups water

3 cups whole wheat flour

¾ cup soy flour

¾ cup ground flaxseed, or flaxseed meal

3 Tbsp. flaxseed

3 Tbsp. sesame seeds

3 Tbsp. poppy seeds

4½ Tbsp. yeast

1 Tbsp. sea salt

1 cup unsweetened applesauce

½ cup honey

¼ cup olive oil

About 5 cups unbleached white flour

Tip:

This is not a fast, easy recipe, but if you like to make a nutritious bread, this is for you. Making good bread takes practice, so keep trying. Be sure to knead it long enough. Like most baked goods, this bread is great right out of the oven.

1. In microwave-safe bowl, microwave oatmeal mixed with water to about 120–130°.

2. In the bowl of a heavy stand mixer with dough hook, combine whole wheat flour, soy flour, ground flaxseed or meal, seeds, yeast, and salt. Stir to mix.

3. Add applesauce, honey, and oil. Mix by hand.

4. Add hot water with oatmeal. Mix by hand.

5. When blended, start mixing with dough hook of mixer and continue for about 3 minutes.

6. Slowly add white flour until dough comes away from sides of bowl and becomes smooth and elastic.

7. Cover dough in bowl and place in a warm spot. Let rise until about double in size, about 1½–2 hours.

8. Punch dough down. Turn onto countertop. Divide evenly into 4 pieces.

9. Shape into 4 loaves. Place in 2½ × 4½ × 8½ loaf pans that have been generously sprayed with non-stick cooking spray.

10. Cover and place in a warm spot. Allow to rise until nearly double in size, about 1½–2 hours.

11. Bake at 350° for 25 minutes, or until tops of loaves are golden.

12. Remove from pans and cool on rack.

Per Serving

Calories 91, Kilojoules 381, Protein 3 g,

Carbohydrates 16 g, Total Fat 2 g, Saturated Fat 0.4 g,

Monounsaturated Fat 1 g, Polyunsaturated Fat 0.6 g,

Cholesterol 0 mg, Sodium 104 mg, Fiber 2 g

Quick Pizza Dough

Lebanon, PA
Makes 2 10" pizza crusts (6 slices/ pizza; 1 slice/serving)

Prep. Time: 10 minutes ❧ *Rising Time: 5 minutes* ❧ *Baking Time: 20 minutes*

I Tbsp. yeast
I cup warm water
I Tbsp. sugar
½ tsp. salt
2 Tbsp. canola oil
1 ¼ cups all-purpose flour
1 ¼ cups whole wheat flour

1. In a good-sized bowl, dissolve yeast in water.

2. Stir in sugar, salt, and oil.

3. Add enough of each flour to make a fairly stiff dough.

4. Cover bowl and set in warm place. Let dough rise 5 minutes.

5. Turn dough onto countertop. Knead until smooth and elastic, using whatever you need of remaining flour.

6. Spray 2 10" pizza pans with non-stick cooking spray. Press dough onto pans, stretching as needed.

7. Spread with your favorite low-calorie toppings.

8. Bake at 400–425° for about 20 minutes, or until lightly browned.

Tip:

We like to top our pizzas with caramelized onions and sweet bell pepper. Slice 2 large onions and chop a large red or green pepper. Put a tablespoon or less olive oil in a large non-stick skillet. Stir in onion and pepper. Cook on low heat, covered, for 45–60 minutes. Stir occasionally. When onions are golden and as tender as you like them, remove from heat and season with a bit of balsamic vinegar. Spread over pizza crust.

Per Serving (without toppings)

Calories 112, Kilojoules 469, Protein 3 g,
Carbohydrates 20 g, Total Fat 2 g, Saturated Fat 0.2 g,
Monounsaturated Fat 1.7 g, Polyunsaturated Fat 0.1 g,
Cholesterol 0 mg, Sodium 99 mg, Fiber 2 g

Sour Cream Corn Bread

Edwina Stoltzfus, Narvon, PA
Makes 9 servings

Prep. Time: 15 minutes ⚜ *Baking Time: 15–20 minutes*

Egg substitute equivalent to 1 egg, or
2 egg whites, beaten
¼ cup skim milk
2 Tbsp. canola oil
1 cup fat-free sour cream
¾ cup cornmeal
½ cup whole wheat flour
½ cup flour
¼ cup sugar
2 tsp. baking powder
½ tsp. baking soda

1. Place egg substitute in good-sized mixing bowl and beat.

2. Add milk, oil, and sour cream and combine well.

3. In a separate bowl, combine all dry ingredients.

4. Add dry ingredients to wet ones. Mix together just until moistened.

5. Spoon into 8″ square baking pan, sprayed lightly with non-stick cooking spray.

6. Bake at 375° 15–20 minutes, or until tester inserted in center comes out clean.

Serving Suggestion:
Serve alongside your favorite stew or chili.

Per Serving

Calories 170, Kilojoules 711, Protein 4 g,
Carbohydrates 26 g, Total Fat 5 g, Saturated Fat 2 g,
Monounsaturated Fat 2 g, Polyunsaturated Fat 1 g,
Cholesterol 8 mg, Sodium 185 mg, Fiber 2 g

Spelt Tortillas

Shari Ladd, Hudson, MI
Makes 10 servings

Prep. Time: 5–7 minutes ⚮ Chilling Time: 4–24 hours ⚮
Warming Time: 1–2 hours ⚮ Cooking Time: 40 seconds

2 cups spelt flour
½ tsp. sea salt
3 Tbsp. canola oil
½ cup water

1. Mix all ingredients together in bowl.

2. Place dough on lightly floured countertop. Knead until smooth.

3. Return dough to bowl. Cover. Refrigerate 4–24 hours.

4. When ready to use, bring dough to room temperature.

5. Divide into 10 pieces. Roll each very thin on dry surface. (No need to use more flour.)

6. Heat skillet, preferably cast iron, until hot. Reduce to medium-high heat.

7. Place tortilla in hot skillet. Fry until bubbly, about 20 seconds.

8. Flip and fry other side, again about 20 seconds.

Tip:
You can use whole wheat flour instead of spelt flour if you wish.

Per Serving
Calories 114, Kilojoules 477, Protein 2 g, Carbohydrates 15 g, Total Fat 5 g, Saturated Fat 0.5 g, Monounsaturated Fat 2.5 g, Polyunsaturated Fat 2 g, Cholesterol 0 mg, Sodium 116 mg, Fiber 2.5 g

Soups, Chilies, and Chowders

Chicken Noodle Soup

Mary Martins, Fairbank, IA
Makes 12 servings

Prep. Time: 1 hour ⚘ *Cooking Time: 3–3¼ hours*

4-lb. stewing chicken, skin removed and cut up

2 quarts water

2 14½-oz. cans low-fat low-sodium chicken broth

5 celery ribs, coarsely chopped, divided

3 medium carrots, sliced, divided

2 medium onions, quartered, divided

⅔ cup coarsely chopped green bell sweet pepper, divided

½ tsp. pepper

1 bay leaf

2 tsp. salt

8 oz. uncooked whole wheat pasta

1. In large stockpot, combine chicken, water, broth, half the celery, half the carrots, half the onions, half the green pepper, ½ teaspoon pepper, and bay leaf. Bring to a boil.

2. Reduce heat. Cover and simmer 2½ hours, or until chicken is tender.

3. Meanwhile, chop remaining onion. Set aside.

4. Remove chicken from broth. When cool enough to handle, remove meat from bones and cut into bite-size pieces. Discard bones and skin. Set chicken aside. (This will equal about 3 lb. cooked meat.)

5. Strain broth and skim fat.

6. Return broth to kettle. Add salt, chopped onion, and remaining celery, carrots, and green pepper.

7. Bring to a boil. Reduce heat. Cover and simmer 10–12 minutes, or until vegetables are crisp-tender.

8. Add pasta and chicken.

9. Cover and simmer 12–15 minutes, or until pasta is tender.

Per Serving

Calories 229, Kilojoules 958, Protein 28 g, Carbohydrates 19 g, Total Fat 4 g, Saturated Fat 1 g, Monounsaturated Fat 2 g, Polyunsaturated Fat 1 g, Cholesterol 80 mg, Sodium 152 mg, Fiber 3 g

Chicken and Vegetable Soup

SLOW COOKER

Hope Comerford, Clinton Township, MI
Makes 4–6 servings

Prep. Time: 15 minutes ❦ *Cooking Time: 7–8 hours* ❦ *Ideal slow cooker size: 5-qt.*

1 lb. boneless skinless chicken, cut into bite-sized pieces

2 celery ribs, diced

1 small yellow squash, diced

4 oz. sliced mushrooms

2 large carrots, diced

1 medium onion, chopped

2 Tbsp. garlic powder

1 Tbsp. onion powder

1 Tbsp. basil

½ tsp. no-salt seasoning

1 tsp. salt

Black pepper to taste

32 oz. low-sodium chicken stock

1. Place the chicken, vegetables, and spices into the crock. Pour the chicken stock over the top.

2. Cover and cook on low for 7–8 hours, or until vegetables are tender.

Per Serving

Calories 152, Kilojoules 636, Protein 21 g, Carbohydrates 9 g, Total Fat 4 g, Saturated Fat 1 g, Monounsaturated Fat 1 g, Polyunsaturated Fat 1 g, Cholesterol 53 mg, Sodium 490 mg, Fiber 2.5 g

Chicken Tortilla Soup

SLOW COOKER

Becky Fixel, Grosse Pointe Farms, MI
Makes 10–12 servings

Prep. Time: 5 minutes & *Cooking Time: 7–8 hours* & *Ideal slow cooker size: 5-qt.*

2 lb. boneless skinless chicken breast

32 oz. gluten-free chicken stock

14 oz. verde sauce

10-oz. can diced tomatoes with lime juice

15-oz. can sweet corn, drained

1 Tbsp. minced garlic

1 small onion, diced

1 Tbsp. chili pepper

½ tsp. fresh ground pepper

½ tsp. salt

½ tsp. oregano

1 Tbsp. dried jalapeño slices

1. Add all ingredients to your slow cooker.

2. Cook on low for 7–8 hours.

3. Approximately 30 minutes before the end, remove your chicken and shred it into small pieces.

Serving suggestion:

Top with a dollop of non-fat plain Greek yogurt, shredded cheese, fresh jalapeños, or fresh cilantro.

Per Serving

Calories 159, Kilojoules 667, Protein 19 g,
Carbohydrates 12 g, Total Fat 4 g, Saturated Fat 1 g,
Monounsaturated Fat 1 g, Polyunsaturated Fat 1 g,
Cholesterol 53 mg, Sodium 472 mg, Fiber 2 g

Southwestern Chili

SLOW COOKER

Colleen Heatwole, Burton, MI
Makes 12 servings

Prep. Time: 30 minutes   ♣   Cooking Time: 6–8 hours   ♣   Ideal slow cooker size: 6- or 7-qt.

32-oz. can of whole tomatoes

15-oz. jar salsa

15-oz. can low-sodium chicken broth

1 cup barley

3 cups water

1 tsp. chili powder

1 tsp. ground cumin

15-oz. can black beans

15-oz. can whole kernel corn

3 cups cooked chicken, chopped

1 cup low-fat shredded cheddar cheese, optional

Low-fat sour cream, optional

1. Combine all ingredients in slow cooker except for optional cheese and sour cream.

2. Cover and cook on low for 6–8 hours.

3. Serve with optional cheese and sour cream on each bowl.

Per Serving (without optional ingredients)
Calories 286, Kilojoules 1199, Protein 22 g,
Carbohydrates 33 g, Total Fat 8 g, Saturated Fat 4 g,
Monounsaturated Fat 1 g, Polyunsaturated Fat 1 g,
Cholesterol 43 mg, Sodium 545 mg, Fiber 8 g

Pumpkin Chili

SLOW COOKER

Hope Comerford, Clinton Township, MI
Makes 8 servings

Prep. Time: 10 minutes ⚜ *Cooking Time: 7–8 hours* ⚜ *Ideal slow cooker size: 6-qt.*

16-oz. can kidney beans, drained and rinsed

16-oz. can black beans, drained and rinsed

1 large onion, chopped

½ green pepper, chopped

1 lb. ground turkey, browned

15-oz. can pumpkin puree

4 cups fresh chopped tomatoes

3 Tbsp. garlic powder

1 Tbsp. ancho chili powder

1 tsp. salt

2 tsp. cumin

¼ tsp. pepper

4 Tbsp. gluten-free beef bouillon granules

5 cups water

1. Place the kidney beans, black beans, onion, and pepper in the crock.

2. Crumble the ground turkey over the top and spoon the pumpkin puree on top of that.

3. Add in the remaining ingredients and stir.

4. Cover and cook on low for 7–8 hours.

Serving suggestion:
Garnish with pumpkin seeds.

Per Serving

Calories 276, Kilojoules 1158, Protein 26 g, Carbohydrates 42 g, Total Fat 8 g, Saturated Fat 0.5 g, Monounsaturated Fat 0.2 g, Polyunsaturated Fat 0.5 g, Cholesterol 28 mg, Sodium 2274 mg, Fiber 12g

Turkey Chili

Julette Rush, Harrisonburg, VA
Makes 5 servings

Prep. Time: 15 minutes ⚘ *Cooking Time: 30 minutes*

½ lb. ground turkey breast

1 cup chopped onions

½ cup chopped green bell sweet pepper

½ cup chopped red bell sweet pepper

14½-oz. can diced tomatoes, no salt added, undrained

15-oz. can solid-pack pumpkin

15½-oz. can pinto beans, rinsed and drained

½ cup water

2 tsp. chili powder

½ tsp. garlic powder

¼ tsp. black pepper

¾ tsp. ground cumin

14½-oz. can low-sodium, fat-free chicken broth

1 cup low-fat shredded cheddar cheese

1. In large stockpot, sauté turkey, onions, and bell peppers until turkey is browned and vegetables are softened.

2. Mix in tomatoes, pumpkin, beans, water, seasonings, and broth. Reduce heat to low.

3. Cover and simmer 20 minutes. Stir occasionally.

4. Top individual servings with cheese.

Per Serving

Calories 232, Kilojoules 971, Protein 24 g, Carbohydrates 28 g, Total Fat 3 g, Saturated Fat 1.6 g, Monounsaturated Fat 0.8 g, Polyunsaturated Fat 0.6 g, Cholesterol 25 mg, Sodium 375 mg, Fiber 9 g

Turkey Rice Soup

Janeen L. Zimmerman, Denver, PA
Makes 10 servings

Prep. Time: 20 minutes ❧ *Cooking Time: 40 minutes*

4 celery ribs, sliced thin

1 onion, chopped

2 Tbsp. olive oil

4 carrots, shredded

⅓ cup whole wheat pastry flour

½ tsp. pepper

2 cups skim milk

4 cups raw wild rice, cooked according to package directions

2⅔ cups raw brown rice, cooked according to package directions

3 cups cooked turkey

3 Tbsp. low-sodium chicken bouillon granules

8 cups water

2 cups low-fat grated cheese, optional, not included in analyses

1. Sauté celery and onion in olive oil.

2. Add carrots. Cook and stir 1–2 minutes.

3. Remove cooked vegetables from pot. Set aside.

4. Combine flour, pepper, and milk in stockpot. Bring to almost boiling, stirring frequently until thickened. Do not scorch or curdle milk.

5. Meanwhile, cook 2 kinds of rice according to package directions.

6. Add both kinds of cooked rice, cooked turkey, bouillon granules, celery mixture, water, and cheese if you wish, to thickened creamy base in stockpot.

7. Cover. Heat thoroughly and serve.

Per Serving

Calories 223, Kilojoules 933, Protein 12 g, Carbohydrates 35 g, Total Fat 4 g, Saturated Fat 0.6 g, Monounsaturated Fat 2.4 g, Polyunsaturated Fat 1 g, Cholesterol 15 mg, Sodium 95 mg, Fiber 4 g

Ham and Bean Soup

Susie Nisley, Millersburg, OH
Makes 10 servings

Prep. Time: 20 minutes ⚜ *Soaking Time: 2 hours* ⚜ *Cooking Time: 1–1½ hours*

1 lb. dry navy beans
1 lb. extra-lean ham, diced
1 green bell sweet pepper, diced
1 small onion, chopped
Half a carrot, diced
1 medium potato, unpeeled and diced
1 cup tomato juice, no salt added
2 tsp. garlic powder
½ tsp. cumin
½ tsp. black pepper
1 tsp. Mrs. Dash, or other salt-free seasoning
1 bunch fresh cilantro, chopped

1. Cover beans with water in large stockpot. Soak 2 hours.

2. Drain beans. Cover beans with fresh water again in stockpot.

3. Add ham. Cover and cook 30 minutes.

4. Stir in remaining ingredients, except cilantro.

5. Cover. Cook another 30 minutes, or until vegetables are cooked to your liking.

6. Stir in chopped fresh cilantro just before serving.

Per Serving
Calories 231, Kilojoules 967, Protein 19 g,
Carbohydrates 35 g, Total Fat 2 g, Saturated Fat 0.4 g,
Monounsaturated Fat 0.6 g, Polyunsaturated Fat 1 g,
Cholesterol 20 mg, Sodium 490 mg, Fiber 12 g

Oven-Baked Bean Soup

Esther H. Becker, Gordonville, PA
Makes 8 servings

Soaking Time: 8 hours or overnight   ❧   *Prep. Time: 30 minutes*   ❧   *Cooking/Baking Time: 2–2¼ hours*

8 oz. (about 1¼ cups) dried white beans

Water to cover

3 cups low-fat, low-sodium chicken broth

1 onion, diced

2 cups raw sweet potatoes (about 2 medium potatoes), diced

1 cup green bell sweet pepper, diced

¼ tsp. ground cloves

¼ tsp. black pepper

½ tsp. dried thyme

½ cup ketchup

¼ cup molasses

1. Soak beans in water overnight. Drain and rinse. Place drained beans in large stockpot.

2. Cover with water. Cover pot. Cook on top of stove for 30 minutes. Drain.

3. Preheat oven to 375°.

4. Place beans in ovenproof Dutch oven, or small roasting pan, along with all but the ketchup and molasses.

5. Cover and bake until beans and sweet potatoes are tender, about 1½ hours.

6. Stir in ketchup, molasses, and more water if necessary.

7. Bake until heated through.

Per Serving

Calories 185, Kilojoules 774, Protein 9 g,
Carbohydrates 37 g, Total Fat trace, Saturated Fat trace,
Monounsaturated Fat trace, Polyunsaturated Fat trace,
Cholesterol 2 mg, Sodium 250 mg, Fiber 6 g

Beef Mushroom Barley Soup

Becky Frey, Lebanon, PA
Makes 8 servings

Prep Time: 20 minutes ⚬ *Cooking Time: 2¼ hours*

1 lb. boneless beef chuck, cubed
½ Tbsp. olive oil
2 cups chopped onion
½ cup sliced celery
1 cup sliced carrots
1 lb. fresh mushrooms, sliced
2 cloves garlic, crushed
½ tsp. dried thyme, optional
8 cups low-fat, low-sodium beef broth, or
2 14½-oz. cans
½ cup uncooked pearl barley
½ tsp. freshly ground pepper
3 Tbsp. chopped fresh parsley, or
1 Tbsp. dried parsley

1. In large saucepan, brown beef on all sides in oil. Remove beef and set aside.

2. Add onion, celery, and carrots to oil in saucepan. Sauté over medium heat about 5 minutes.

3. Add mushrooms, garlic, and thyme. Cook and stir about 2 minutes.

4. Add meat and all remaining ingredients, except the parsley, to saucepan. Bring to a boil.

5. Cover. Reduce heat and simmer about 2 hours, or until beef and barley are tender. If stew becomes too thick, add more water or broth.

6. Add parsley and serve piping hot.

Per Serving

Calories 175, Kilojoules 732, Protein 16 g,
Carbohydrates 17 g, Total Fat 5 g, Saturated Fat 1.5 g,
Monounsaturated Fat 2.5 g, Polyunsaturated Fat 1 g,
Cholesterol 32 mg, Sodium 232 mg, Fiber 4 g

Minestrone

Elva Bare, Lancaster, PA
Makes 14 servings

Prep. Time: 30 minutes   Cooking Time: 40–60 minutes

1 lb. 95%-lean ground beef

½ cup chopped onion

1 clove garlic, cut fine

1 celery rib, chopped

2 14-oz. cans reduced-sodium fat-free chicken broth

2 14-oz. cans reduced-sodium fat-free beef broth

14-oz. can diced tomatoes, undrained, no salt added

14-oz. can Italian tomatoes, undrained, no salt added

1½ cups sliced zucchini

16-oz. can kidney beans, rinsed and drained

16-oz. can black beans, rinsed and drained

1½ cups fresh, or frozen, corn

1½ cups shredded cabbage

1–2 tsp. no-salt Italian seasoning

½ cup uncooked whole wheat elbow macaroni

1. In large stockpot, sauté beef, onion, garlic, and celery until beef is no longer pink.

2. Stir in broths, tomatoes, zucchini, beans, corn, cabbage, and seasoning.

3. Cover. Bring to a boil.

4. Add macaroni. Stir and reduce heat.

5. Cover and simmer 20 minutes, or until macaroni is soft.

Per Serving

Calories 168, Kilojoules 703, Protein 15 g, Carbohydrates 23 g, Total Fat 2 g, Saturated Fat 1 g, Monounsaturated Fat 0.7 g, Polyunsaturated Fat 0.3 g, Cholesterol 21 mg, Sodium 262 mg, Fiber 6 g

Quick and Hearty Vegetable Soup

Berenice M. Wagner, Dodge City, KS
Sherri Grindle, Goshen, IN
Makes 8 servings

Prep. Time: 10 minutes ♣ Cooking Time: 35–40 minutes

½ lb. 95%-lean ground beef
½ cup chopped onion
1 clove garlic, minced
5 cups water
14½-oz. can diced tomatoes, undrained, no salt added
¾ cup uncooked quick-cooking barley
2 low-salt beef bouillon cubes
½ cup sliced carrots
½ tsp. crushed dried basil
1 bay leaf
9-oz. pkg. frozen mixed vegetables

1. In 4-quart saucepan, brown meat. Drain off drippings.

2. Add onion and garlic. Cook until onion is tender.

3. Stir in remaining ingredients, except frozen vegetables.

4. Cover and bring to a boil. Reduce heat. Simmer, covered, 10 minutes, stirring occasionally.

5. Add frozen vegetables. Cook 10 minutes longer. Add more water if soup becomes too thick.

Per Serving

Calories 139, Kilojoules 582, Protein 10 g,
Carbohydrates 21 g, Total Fat 2 g, Saturated Fat 1.2 g,
Monounsaturated Fat 0.6 g, Polyunsaturated Fat 0.2 g,
Cholesterol 17 mg, Sodium 218 mg, Fiber 5 g

Garden Vegetable Soup with Pasta

Jan McDowell, New Holland, PA
Makes 6 servings

Prep. Time: 20 minutes   &   Cooking Time: 30 minutes

I Tbsp. olive oil

I chopped onion

I tsp. chopped garlic

I small zucchini, chopped

½ lb. fresh mushrooms, sliced or chopped

I bell sweet pepper, chopped

24-oz. can chopped tomatoes, no salt added, undrained, or 10-12 whole tomatoes, peeled and chopped

I Tbsp. fresh basil

2 cups water

3 reduced-sodium vegetable bouillon cubes

2 cups whole-grain rotini, cooked

Dash of hot sauce, optional

1. Heat olive oil in 4-quart saucepan.

2. Sauté onion and garlic in oil until tender.

3. Add zucchini, mushrooms, bell pepper, tomatoes, basil, water, and bouillon.

4. Bring to a boil. Cover and simmer 10 minutes.

5. Meanwhile, cook rotini and drain. Add to soup.

6. Cover and heat through.

7. Pass hot sauce to be added to individual servings, if desired.

Per Serving
Calories 123, Kilojoules 515, Protein 4 g,
Carbohydrates 20 g, Total Fat 3 g, Saturated Fat 0.5 g,
Monounsaturated Fat 1.5 g, Polyunsaturated Fat 1 g,
Cholesterol trace, Sodium 61 mg, Fiber 5 g

Herbed Lentil Soup

Marcia S. Myer, Manheim, PA
Makes 6 servings

Prep. Time: 15 minutes   *Cooking Time: 1 hour*

2 large onions, chopped

1 carrot, chopped

½ tsp. dried thyme

½ tsp. dried marjoram

3 cups low-sodium, fat-free chicken, or vegetable, broth

1 cup uncooked lentils

¼ cup chopped fresh parsley

1 lb. canned tomatoes, no salt added, undrained

¼ cup sherry, optional (not included in analyses)

⅔ cup grated low-fat cheese, optional (not included in analyses)

1. Spray bottom of large stockpot with non-stick cooking spray. Sauté onions and carrot 3–5 minutes.

2. Add thyme and marjoram.

3. Add broth, lentils, parsley, and tomatoes.

4. Cover and simmer about 45 minutes, or until lentils are tender.

5. Stir in sherry, if you wish.

6. Top each individual serving of soup with 1½ Tbsp. grated cheese, if you wish.

Per Serving
Calories 160, Kilojoules 669, Protein 11 g,
Carbohydrates 27 g, Total Fat 1 g, Saturated Fat 0.3 g,
Monounsaturated Fat 0.5 g, Polyunsaturated Fat 0.2 g,
Cholesterol 3 mg, Sodium 111 mg, Fiber 12 g

Hearty Lentil and Barley Soup

Sherri Grindle, Goshen, IN
Makes 10 servings

Prep. Time: 15 minutes ❦ *Cooking Time: 65 minutes*

2 ribs celery, thinly sliced

1 medium onion, chopped

1 clove garlic, minced

2 Tbsp. olive oil

6 cups water

28-oz. can diced tomatoes, no salt added, undrained, or 10-12 whole tomatoes, peeled and diced

¾ cup uncooked lentils, rinsed

¾ cup uncooked pearl barley

2 Tbsp. (or 3 cubes) low-sodium chicken bouillon granules

1½ tsp. fresh chopped oregano

1½ tsp. fresh chopped rosemary

¼ tsp. pepper

1 cup thinly sliced carrots

1 cup (4 oz.) shredded low-fat Swiss cheese, optional

1. In Dutch oven or soup kettle, sauté celery, onion, and garlic in oil until tender.

2. Add water, tomatoes, lentils, barley, bouillon, oregano, rosemary, and pepper.

3. Bring to a boil. Reduce heat, cover, and simmer 40 minutes, or until lentils and barley are almost tender.

4. Add carrots. Cover and simmer 15 minutes, or until carrots, lentils, and barley are tender.

5. If you wish, sprinkle each serving with 1 rounded Tbsp. cheese.

Per Serving (without optional shredded cheese)
Calories 156, Kilojoules 653, Protein 6 g,
Carbohydrates 27 g, Total Fat 3 g, Saturated Fat 0.5 g,
Monounsaturated Fat 2 g, Polyunsaturated Fat 0.5 g,
Cholesterol 0 mg, Sodium 236 mg, Fiber 9 g

Wild Rice Mushroom Soup

Kelly Amos, Pittsboro, NC
Makes 4 servings

Prep. Time: 15–20 minutes ❧ *Cooking Time: 35 minutes*

1 Tbsp. olive oil

Half a white onion, chopped

¼ cup chopped celery

¼ cup chopped carrots

1½ cups sliced fresh white mushrooms

½ cup white wine, or ½ cup low-sodium, fat-free chicken broth

2½ cups low-sodium, fat-free chicken broth

1 cup fat-free half-and-half

2 Tbsp. flour

¾ tsp. fresh chopped thyme

Black pepper

1 cup cooked wild rice

1. Put olive oil in stockpot and heat. Carefully add chopped onion, celery, and carrots. Cook until tender.

2. Add mushrooms, white wine, and chicken broth.

3. Cover and heat through.

4. In a bowl, blend half-and-half, flour, thyme, and pepper. Then stir in cooked wild rice.

5. Pour rice mixture into hot stockpot with vegetables.

6. Cook over medium heat. Stir continually until thickened and bubbly.

Per Serving

Calories 170, Kilojoules 711, Protein 7 g,
Carbohydrates 20 g, Total Fat 5 g, Saturated Fat 1 g,
Monounsaturated Fat 3 g, Polyunsaturated Fat 1 g,
Cholesterol 6 mg, Sodium 190 mg, Fiber 1.5 g

Creamy Potato Chowder

Sylvia Beiler, Lowville, NY
Makes 4 servings

Prep. Time: 5 minutes ⚬ *Cooking Time: 30–35 minutes*

1 tsp. olive oil

½ cup chopped onion

½ cup chopped celery

2 garlic cloves, minced

1 carrot, diced

2 cups cubed unpeeled potatoes

2 Tbsp. flour

2 cups skim milk

1½ cup reduced sodium, low-fat chicken, or vegetable, broth

1 cup corn

Pepper to taste

1. Heat oil in large saucepan over medium heat. Add onion, celery, and garlic. Sauté 2 minutes.

2. Add carrot and potatoes. Sauté 3 minutes.

3. Sprinkle flour over carrot and potatoes. Cook 1 minute, stirring continually.

4. Add remaining ingredients and bring to a boil.

5. Lower heat, cover, and simmer 20–25 minutes, or until carrot and potatoes are soft.

6. To thicken soup, mash vegetables somewhat before serving.

Per Serving

Calories 181, Kilojoules 757, Protein 9 g,
Carbohydrates 32 g, Total Fat 2 g, Saturated Fat 0.5 g,
Monounsaturated Fat 1 g, Polyunsaturated Fat 0.5 g,
Cholesterol 4 mg, Sodium 131 mg, Fiber 4 g

Low-Fat Broccoli Soup

Carolyn Snader, Ephrata, PA
Joyce Nolt, Richland, PA
Makes 4 servings

Prep. Time: 15–20 minutes ♣ Cooking Time: 12 minutes

1 lb. (about 5 cups) chopped fresh, or frozen, broccoli

½ cup chopped onion

14½-oz. can low-sodium, fat-free chicken, or vegetable, broth

2 Tbsp. cornstarch

12-oz. can evaporated skim milk

½ cup low-fat cheddar cheese, grated

1. In a good-sized stockpot, cook broccoli and onion in chicken broth 5–10 minutes.

2. Carefully puree half of mixture in blender.

3. Stir back into remaining broccoli in stockpot.

4. Place cornstarch in jar with tight-fitting lid. Pour in a little milk. Cover and shake until smooth.

5. Pour rest of milk into jar. Cover and shake until smooth. Stir into soup.

6. Cover and simmer 2 minutes.

7. Top each individual serving with 2 Tbsp. grated cheese.

Per Serving

Calories 165, Kilojoules 690, Protein 15 g,
Carbohydrates 22 g, Total Fat 2 g, Saturated Fat 1 g,
Monounsaturated Fat 0.4 g, Polyunsaturated Fat 0.6 g,
Cholesterol 8 mg, Sodium 285 mg, Fiber 3 g

Flavorful Tomato Soup

Shari Ladd, Hudson, MI
Makes 4 servings

Prep. Time: 10 minutes   Cooking Time: 20 minutes

2 Tbsp. chopped onions

1 Tbsp. extra-virgin olive oil

3 Tbsp. flour

2 tsp. sugar

½ tsp. pepper

¼ tsp. dried basil

½ tsp. dried oregano

¼ tsp. dried thyme

1 quart stewed tomatoes, no salt added, undrained

2 cups skim milk

1. Sauté onions in oil in stockpot.

2. Stir in flour and seasonings.

3. Stir in stewed tomatoes, stirring constantly. Bring to a boil and boil 1 minute.

4. Add 2 cups milk. If soup is too thick, add a little water. Stir well.

5. Simmer 10 minutes but do not boil.

Per Serving

Calories 174, Kilojoules 728, Protein 7 g, Carbohydrates 30 g, Total Fat 3 g, Saturated Fat 0.5 g, Monounsaturated Fat 2 g, Polyunsaturated Fat 0.5 g, Cholesterol 2 mg, Sodium 152 mg, Fiber 4 g

Main Dishes

Salads

Strawberry Spinach Salad with Turkey or Chicken

Genelle Taylor, Perrysburg, OH
Makes 4 main-dish servings

Prep. Time: 45–60 minutes

1 lb. asparagus spears

¼ cup poppy seed dressing

1 tsp. grated orange peel

1 Tbsp. orange juice

8 cups torn fresh spinach, or assorted greens

2 cups sliced fresh strawberries and/or whole blueberries

¾ lb. cooked turkey or grilled chicken, cubed

¼ cup pecan halves

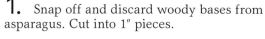

1. Snap off and discard woody bases from asparagus. Cut into 1″ pieces.

2. In a 1-quart microwaveable covered dish, cook asparagus with 2 tablespoons of water for 5–7 minutes, or until tender-crisp. Drain. Rinse with cold water; drain again.

3. In a medium bowl, stir together poppy seed dressing, orange peel, and orange juice. Set aside.

4. In a salad bowl, combine asparagus, greens, berries, and turkey or chicken. Add dressing mixture and toss.

5. Top with pecans just before serving.

Per Serving
Calories 288, Kilojoules 1205, Protein 29 g, Carbohydrates 13 g, Total Fat 13 g, Saturated Fat 2 g, Monounsaturated Fat 8 g, Polyunsaturated Fat 3 g, Cholesterol 73 mg, Sodium 200 mg, Fiber 5 g

Grilled Fiesta Chicken Salad

Liz Clapper, Lancaster, PA
Makes 4 main-dish servings

Prep. Time: 25 minutes   ❧   Cooking Time: 10 minutes

1 head Bibb lettuce

1 head red leaf lettuce

1 cup shredded carrots

1 medium tomato, diced

2 green onions, chopped

1 lb. boneless skinless chicken breasts

1 tsp. chili powder

1 sweet red pepper

1 Tbsp. olive oil

1 cup thawed frozen corn

½ cup shredded low-fat cheddar cheese

8 Tbsp. fat-free ranch dressing

2 whole wheat pita breads, 4" diameter

1. Tear up heads of lettuce and toss together in a large bowl. Top with shredded carrots, diced tomato, and chopped green onions.

2. Season chicken with chili powder. Grill chicken 3–4 minutes on each side.

3. Meanwhile, dice red pepper. Toss with olive oil and cook in a medium skillet over medium heat for 2 minutes.

4. Add corn and cook for 1 more minute.

5. When chicken has cooled to room temperature, dice chicken.

6. Top salad with diced chicken.

7. Spoon corn and pepper over top.

8. Sprinkle with cheese. Drizzle each salad with 2 Tbsp. dressing.

9. Grill whole wheat pitas for 2–3 minutes each side. Cut into fourths. Serve 2 wedges with each individual salad.

Tip:

You can bake pitas at 375° in oven for 10 minutes instead of grilling.

Per Serving

Calories 337, Kilojoules 1410, Protein 36 g, Carbohydrates 33 g, Total Fat 8 g, Saturated Fat 2 g, Monounsaturated Fat 4 g, Polyunsaturated Fat 2 g, Cholesterol 71 mg, Sodium 512 mg, Fiber 6 g

Italian Pasta Salad

Monica Kehr, Portland, MI
Makes 8 main-dish servings

Prep. Time: 20 minutes ⚬ *Cooking Time: 15 minutes*

14½-oz. box whole wheat rotini

4 medium tomatoes, diced

1 medium red bell sweet pepper, diced

1 medium yellow bell sweet pepper, diced

1 medium cucumber, diced

Half a red onion, sliced thin

2 cups fresh broccoli florets, chopped

⅓ cup sliced black olives

1 tsp. salt-free Italian seasoning

¼ cup olive oil

½ cup red wine vinegar

8 tsp. grated Parmesan cheese

1. Cook pasta according to directions. Rinse with cool water.

2. Mix all ingredients, except seasoning, olive oil, vinegar, and cheese, in a large bowl.

3. Combine seasoning, oil, and vinegar in another bowl, or a jar with a tight-fitting lid.

4. Serve pasta, with each individual serving topped with 1½ Tbsp. dressing and 1 tsp. grated cheese.

Tip:

Since the dressing and cheese aren't mixed in with everything else, the pasta salad keeps longer so leftovers are good.

Per Serving

Calories 312, Kilojoules 1305, Protein 9 g,
Carbohydrates 47 g, Total Fat 10 g, Saturated Fat 1.5 g,
Monounsaturated Fat 6 g, Polyunsaturated Fat 2.5 g,
Cholesterol 1 mg, Sodium 133 mg, Fiber 8 g

Chicken

Honey Baked Chicken

Rhoda Nissley, Parkesburg, PA
Makes 10 servings

Prep. Time: 5–10 minutes ⚬ *Baking Time: 1–1¼ hours*

3 lb. chicken pieces, skinned
1 Tbsp. butter, melted
1 Tbsp. olive oil
2 Tbsp. prepared mustard
1 tsp. curry powder
⅓ cup honey
⅓ cup water

1. Preheat oven to 350°.

2. Arrange chicken in a single layer in a shallow, lightly greased baking dish.

3. Combine all other ingredients in a bowl. Pour over chicken.

4. Place in oven, uncovered. Baste chicken with sauce every 15 minutes.

5. Bake until nicely browned and tender, about 1–1¼ hours.

Per Serving

Calories 232, Kilojoules 971, Protein 29 g,
Carbohydrates 10 g, Total Fat 8 g, Saturated Fat 2 g,
Monounsaturated Fat 4 g, Polyunsaturated Fat 2 g,
Cholesterol 98 mg, Sodium 147 mg, Fiber trace

Barbecued Chicken Thighs

Ida H. Goering, Dayton, VA
Makes 6 servings

Prep. Time: 10 minutes ❧ *Marinating Time: 2–4 hours* ❧ *Grilling Time: 15–22 minutes*

6 Tbsp. apple cider vinegar
3 Tbsp. canola oil
3 Tbsp. ketchup
¼ tsp. black pepper
¼ tsp. poultry seasoning
12 boneless skinless chicken thighs

1. Combine all ingredients except chicken thighs in a large bowl.

2. Submerge thighs in sauce in bowl.

3. Marinate 2–4 hours, stirring several times to be sure meat is well covered.

4. Grill over medium heat, turning after 10–15 minutes.

5. Grill another 5–7 minutes. Watch carefully so meat doesn't dry out. Remove from grill earlier if finished.

Per Serving
Calories 273, Kilojoules 1142, Protein 35 g, Carbohydrates 2 g, Total Fat 13 g, Saturated Fat 2 g, Monounsaturated Fat 7 g, Polyunsaturated Fat 4 g, Cholesterol 141 mg, Sodium 242 mg, Fiber trace

Breaded Baked Chicken

Linda Thomas, Sayner, WI
Makes 4 servings

Prep. Time: 10–15 minutes ⚬ *Baking Time: 35–40 minutes*

3 Tbsp. grated Parmesan cheese
½ cup dry bread crumbs
½ tsp. rosemary
½ tsp. dried thyme
¼ tsp. garlic powder
¼ tsp. onion powder
¼ tsp. black pepper
¾ cup low-fat buttermilk
1 lb. skinned chicken pieces

1. Cover a baking sheet with aluminum foil. Spray lightly with non-stick cooking spray.

2. In a shallow dish combine all ingredients except chicken and buttermilk.

3. In a separate shallow bowl, dip chicken in buttermilk.

4. Then roll chicken pieces in dry mixture.

5. Place chicken pieces on baking sheet.

6. Bake at 400° for 35–40 minutes, or until golden brown.

Per Serving
Calories 213, Kilojoules 891, Protein 31 g,
Carbohydrates 13 g, Total Fat 4 g, Saturated Fat 1.5 g,
Monounsaturated Fat 2 g, Polyunsaturated Fat 0.5 g,
Cholesterol 71 mg, Sodium 277 mg, Fiber 1 g

Homemade Chicken Strips

Barb Harvey, Quarryville, PA
Makes 6 servings

Prep. Time: 20 minutes  *Cooking/Baking Time: 20 minutes*

1 cup Italian bread crumbs

2 Tbsp. grated Parmesan cheese

1 garlic clove, minced

2 Tbsp. vegetable oil

6 (about 2 lb. total) boneless skinless chicken breast halves

Honey Mustard Sauce:

2 Tbsp. cornstarch

1 cup water, divided

½ cup honey

¼ cup prepared mustard

1. In plastic bag, mix bread crumbs and cheese.

2. In a small bowl, combine garlic and oil.

3. Flatten chicken to ½" thickness. Cut into 1"-wide strips.

4. Dip each strip in garlic oil.

5. Coat each with crumb mixture. Place on a greased baking sheet without letting the strips touch each other.

6. Bake at 350° for 20 minutes, or until golden brown.

7. Dissolve cornstarch in 1 Tbsp. water in a saucepan.

8. Stir in honey, mustard, and remaining water.

9. Bring to a boil over medium heat, stirring constantly.

10. Serve as a dipping sauce for the chicken fingers.

Per Serving

Calories 382, Kilojoules 1598, Protein 36 g, Carbohydrates 41 g, Total Fat 8 g, Saturated Fat 1.5 g, Monounsaturated Fat 3 g, Polyunsaturated Fat 3.5 g, Cholesterol 84 mg, Sodium 585 mg, Fiber 1.5 g

Chicken Fajitas

Becky Frey, Lebanon, PA
Makes 12 servings

Prep. Time: 20–30 minutes ⚜ *Marinating Time: 15 minutes* ⚜ *Cooking Time: 6–8 minutes*

¼ cup lime juice

1–2 garlic cloves minced

1 tsp. chili powder

½ tsp. ground cumin

3 lb. boneless skinless chicken breasts, cut into ¼" slices

1 large onion, sliced

Half a green bell sweet pepper, slivered

Half a red bell sweet pepper, slivered

12 whole wheat tortillas, 8" in diameter

½ cup salsa

½ cup non-fat sour cream

½ cup your favorite low-fat shredded cheese

1. Combine first four ingredients in a large bowl.

2. Add chicken slices. Stir until chicken is well coated.

3. Marinate for 15 minutes.

4. Cook chicken mixture in large hot non-stick skillet for 3 minutes, or until no longer pink.

5. Stir in onions and peppers. Cook 3–5 minutes, or until done to your liking.

6. Divide mixture evenly among tortillas.

7. Top each with 2 tsp. salsa, 2 tsp. sour cream, and 2 tsp. shredded cheese.

8. Roll up and serve.

Tips:

Partially frozen chicken slices much more easily than completely thawed chicken. If you like a higher heat index, add your favorite hot pepper along with the sweet peppers.

Per Serving

Calories 334, Kilojoules 1397, Protein 34 g, Carbohydrates 30 g, Total Fat 9 g, Saturated Fat 2 g, Monounsaturated Fat 6 g, Polyunsaturated Fat 1 g, Cholesterol 68 mg, Sodium 689 mg, Fiber 6 g

Chicken Rice Bake

Nanci Keatley, Salem, OR
Makes 6 servings

Prep. Time: 20 minutes ⚭ Baking Time: 1½ hours ⚭ Standing Time: 10 minutes

2 lb. boneless skinless chicken breasts,
cut into bite-sized pieces

3½ cups low-sodium chicken broth

1½ cups uncooked brown rice

1 cup chopped celery

1 cup chopped carrots

1 cup finely diced onions

2 cups sliced fresh mushrooms

1½ tsp. salt

1 tsp. pepper

1 tsp. dill weed

1 tsp. garlic, chopped

1. Spray a 2-quart baking dish with non-stick cooking spray.

2. Combine all ingredients in large mixing bowl.

3. Spoon into baking dish. Bake at 350° for 1½ hours.

4. Allow to stand 10 minutes before serving.

Per Serving

Calories 390, Kilojoules 1632, Protein 43 g,
Carbohydrates 45 g, Total Fat 4 g, Saturated Fat 1 g,
Monounsaturated Fat 2 g, Polyunsaturated Fat 1 g,
Cholesterol 88 mg, Sodium 755 mg, Fiber 3.3 g

Easy Enchilada Shredded Chicken

Hope Comerford, Clinton Township, MI
Makes 10–14 servings

Prep. Time: 5 minutes & Cooking Time: 5–6 hours & Ideal slow cooker size: 3- or 5-qt.

SLOW COOKER

5–6 lb. boneless skinless chicken breast

14½-oz. can petite diced tomatoes

1 medium onion, chopped

8 oz. red enchilada sauce

½ tsp. salt

½ tsp. chil powder

½ tsp. basil

½ tsp. garlic powder

¼ tsp. pepper

1. Place chicken in the crock.

2. Add in the remaining ingredients.

3. Cover and cook on low for 5–6 hours.

4. Remove chicken and shred it between two forks. Place the shredded chicken back in the crock and stir to mix in the juices.

Serving suggestion:

Serve over salad, brown rice, quinoa, sweet potatoes, nachos, or soft-shell corn tacos. Add a dollop of yogurt and a sprinkle of fresh cilantro.

Per Serving

Calories 251, Kilojoules 1052, Protein 42 g, Carbohydrates 3 g, Total Fat 6.5 g, Saturated Fat 2 g, Monounsaturated Fat 2 g, Polyunsaturated Fat 1 g, Cholesterol 136 mg, Sodium 339 mg, Fiber 0 g

Asian Style Chicken with Pineapple

Andrea Maher, Dunedin, FL
Makes 6 servings

Prep. Time: 10 minutes ☆ Cooking Time: 6–8 hours ☆ Ideal slow cooker size: 5- or 6-qt.

24 oz. boneless skinless chicken breast, cut into bite size pieces

3 cups pineapple, cubed

¼ cup Bragg's liquid aminos

1 Tbsp. brown sugar

½ cup chopped onion or 2 Tbsp. onion powder

1 cup low-sodium gluten-free chicken broth or stock

½ tsp. ground ginger

2 16-oz. bags frozen Szechuan mixed veggies or any mixed veggies

1. Add all ingredients except for frozen veggies to the slow cooker.

2. Cover and cook on high 3–4 hours or low 6–8 hours.

3. Add frozen veggies in the last 1–2 hours.

Per Serving
Calories 295, Kilojoules 1237, Protein 31 g, Carbohydrates 34 g, Total Fat 4 g, Saturated Fat 1 g, Monounsaturated Fat 1 g, Polyunsaturated Fat 1 g, Cholesterol 80 mg, Sodium 612 mg, Fiber 7 g

Honey-Chicken Stir Fry

Anya Kauffman, Sheldon, WI
Makes 6 servings

Prep. Time: 15 minutes   Cooking Time: 10 minutes

1 lb. boneless skinless chicken breast

2 Tbsp. canola oil, divided

4 cups sliced raw vegetables (your choice of a combination of cabbage, onion, celery, carrots, broccoli, cauliflower, sweet peppers)

Sauce:

1½ cups orange juice

⅔ cup honey

1 Tbsp. low-sodium soy sauce

2 Tbsp. cornstarch

½ tsp. ground ginger

1. Slice chicken breast into thin strips. Set aside.

2. Combine sauce ingredients in a bowl.

3. In a large skillet, stir-fry meat in 1 Tbsp. oil until no longer pink. Remove from skillet and set aside.

4. In remaining oil and in same skillet, stir-fry vegetables on high heat until crisp-tender.

5. Stir in meat and sauce until sauce is somewhat thickened.

Serving suggestion:

Serve over hot brown rice.

Per Serving

Calories 292, Kilojoules 1222, Protein 20 g,
Carbohydrates 40 g, Total Fat 6 g, Saturated Fat 0.5 g,
Monounsaturated Fat 3 g, Polyunsaturated Fat 2.5 g,
Cholesterol 44 mg, Sodium 168 mg, Fiber 2 g

Skinny Chicken Stroganoff

Carol Sherwood, Batavia, NY
Makes 6 servings

Prep. Time: 10–15 minutes ❧ Cooking Time: 20–25 minutes

4 slices turkey bacon, cooked and broken

6 oz. uncooked whole wheat noodles

¾ cup reduced-fat sour cream

¼ cup all-purpose flour

14½-oz. can low-fat low-sodium chicken broth

⅛ tsp. black pepper

1 lb. boneless skinless chicken breasts, cut into ¼" strips

8 oz. sliced fresh mushrooms

1 cup chopped onion

1 clove garlic, pressed

2 Tbsp. snipped fresh parsley

1. Cook bacon until crisp in a large skillet. Remove from pan, break, and set aside.

2. Cook noodles according to package instructions. Drain and keep warm.

3. Meanwhile, in a good-sized bowl, whisk together sour cream and flour until smooth.

4. Gradually whisk in chicken broth until smooth. Stir in pepper. Set aside.

5. Heat skillet that you used for bacon over high heat until hot. Add chicken. Cook, stirring continually for 3 minutes, or until meat is no longer pink. Remove from pan and set aside. Keep warm.

6. Reduce heat to medium. Add mushrooms, onion, and garlic. Cook and stir 3 minutes.

7. Stir in chicken and bacon.

8. Stir in sour cream mixture. Bring to a boil.

9. Reduce heat. Simmer 2 minutes, stirring constantly.

10. Remove from heat. Stir in parsley.

11. Serve over prepared noodles (not included in analyses).

Per Serving

Calories 278, Kilojoules 1163, Protein 26 g,
Carbohydrates 36 g, Total Fat 3 g, Saturated Fat 1 g,
Monounsaturated Fat 1 g, Polyunsaturated Fat 1 g,
Cholesterol 53 mg, Sodium 256 mg, Fiber 4 g

Buffalo Chicken Meatballs

SLOW COOKER

Hope Comerford, Clinton Township, MI
Makes 6 servings

Prep. Time: 20–30 minutes ⚶ *Cooking Time: 6 hours* ⚶ *Ideal slow cooker size: 5- or 6-qt.*

1 ½ lb. ground chicken

¾ cup gluten-free hot sauce of your choice, divided

2 Tbsp. dry minced onion

2 Tbsp. garlic powder

¼ tsp. pepper

1 egg

1 cup gluten-free panko bread crumbs

1 ½–2 Tbsp. coconut oil

2 tsp. gluten-free chicken bouillon granules

1 cup water

2 cups non-fat plain Greek yogurt

2 Tbsp. cornstarch

1. In a bowl, combine the ground chicken, ½ cup hot sauce, minced onion, garlic powder, pepper, egg, and gluten-free panko bread crumbs.

2. Heat the coconut oil in a large skillet over medium-high heat.

3. Roll the chicken mixture into 1½–2" balls. Place them in the skillet, turning them regularly so they're seared on each side.

4. Place the seared meatballs into your crock. Sprinkle them with the chicken bouillon granules and pour in the water.

5. Cover and cook on low for 6 hours.

6. Remove the meatballs in a covered dish to keep them warm.

7. In a bowl, stir together the Greek yogurt, cornstarch, and remaining ¼ cup of hot sauce. Gently whisk this back into your crock with the juices.

8. You can either place your browned meatballs back into the sauce to coat them, or you can serve the meatballs with the sauce spooned over the top.

Serving suggestion:

Serve meatballs over browned rice with a fresh salad on the side. If desired, add more hot sauce to taste.

Per Serving

Calories 349, Kilojoules 1462, Protein 30 g, Carbohydrates 15 g, Total Fat 15 g, Saturated Fat 7 g, Monounsaturated Fat 4 g, Polyunsaturated Fat 2 g, Cholesterol 134 mg, Sodium 735 mg, Fiber 0.5 g

Turkey

Turkey "Spaghetti" Quinoa

Hope Comerford, Clinton Township, MI
Makes 8–10 servings

Prep. Time: 10–15 minutes ⚜ *Cooking Time: 5 hours* ⚜ *Ideal slow cooker size: 5- or 6-qt.*

SLOW COOKER

2 lb. lean ground turkey

½ tsp. salt

⅛ tsp. pepper

1 tsp. garlic powder

1 tsp. onion powder

1 cup quinoa

1 cup chopped onion

1 cup shredded mozzarella cheese (for dairy-free, substitute with dairy-free cheese or leave out)

4 cups tomato sauce

2 cups water

1. Brown turkey with the salt, pepper, garlic powder, and onion powder.

2. Spray crock with non-stick spray.

3. Place ground turkey in bottom of crock. Top with quinoa, onion, and shredded mozzarella.

4. Pour tomato sauce and water into crock. Stir so everything is mixed.

5. Cover and cook on low for 5 hours.

Per Serving

Calories 202, Kilojoules 849, Protein 29 g, Carbohydrates 11 g, Total Fat 5 g, Saturated Fat 3 g, Monounsaturated Fat 1 g, Polyunsaturated Fat 0.2 g, Cholesterol 58 mg, Sodium 799 mg, Fiber 2 g

Spaghetti Pie

Marlene Fonken, Upland, CA
Makes 4 servings

Prep. Time: 15 minutes ⚘ *Cooking/Baking Time: 45 minutes*

4 oz. uncooked thin whole wheat spaghetti, or vermicelli (or 2 cups cooked)

1 Tbsp. olive oil

2 Tbsp. reduced-fat Parmesan cheese

Egg substitute equivalent to 1 egg, or 2 egg whites, beaten

⅔ cup non-fat cottage cheese, or ½ cup non-fat ricotta

1 clove garlic, minced

½ cup diced onion

½ cup diced green or red bell sweet pepper

½ lb. lean ground turkey

1 cup canned tomatoes, no salt added, chopped, undrained

¼ cup tomato paste, no salt added

½ tsp. dried basil

½ tsp. dried oregano

¼ cup low-fat mozzarella cheese, shredded

1. Cook spaghetti according to package directions. Drain. Return to saucepan.

2. Stir oil, Parmesan cheese, and beaten egg substitute or white into cooked spaghetti. Mix well.

3. Spray a glass 8″ pie plate or 7 × 9 baking dish with non-stick cooking spray. Spread spaghetti mixture over bottom and up sides to form a crust.

4. Spread cottage cheese over bottom of crust.

5. In saucepan, cook garlic, onion, pepper, and turkey together until meat loses its pink color. (You may need to add a little water to pan to prevent sticking.)

6. Add tomatoes, tomato paste, basil, and oregano to pan. Cook until heated through.

7. Spoon turkey-tomato mixture over cottage cheese.

8. Bake, uncovered, approximately 20 minutes at 350°.

9. Sprinkle mozzarella cheese on top.

10. Continue to bake another 5 minutes, or until cheese is melted.

Per Serving

Calories 316, Kilojoules 1322, Protein 24 g, Carbohydrates 35 g, Total Fat 9 g, Saturated Fat 2.5 g, Monounsaturated Fat 3.5 g, Polyunsaturated Fat 3 g, Cholesterol 42 mg, Sodium 335 mg, Fiber 5 g

Turkey Quesadillas

Tara P. Detweiler, Pennsburg, PA
Makes 8 servings

Prep. Time: 15 minutes ⚘ *Cooking/Baking Time: 20 minutes*

I lb. ground turkey

4 tsp. olive oil

I large onion, chopped

I red bell sweet pepper, chopped

4 cloves garlic, chopped

I tsp. ground cumin

I tsp. chili powder

I tsp. dried oregano

15-oz. can tomato sauce, no salt added

15½-oz. can kidney, or black, beans, drained and rinsed

8 whole wheat flour tortillas, about 9" in diameter

2 Tbsp. parsley

I tsp. cilantro

½ cup grated low-fat cheddar cheese for topping

1. Cook ground turkey with olive oil and onion in large skillet until turkey is no longer pink.

2. Add red pepper, garlic, and all spices. Cook gently until vegetables are just tender.

3. Stir in tomato sauce and beans. Heat through.

4. Place tortillas on greased cookie sheets. Spoon turkey mixture evenly onto tortillas (approximately ¼ cup per tortilla).

5. Top each with 1 Tbsp. grated cheese.

6. Bake, uncovered, at 400° for 15 minutes.

Per Serving

Calories 358, Kilojoules 1498, Protein 25 g, Carbohydrates 40 g, Total Fat 11 g, Saturated Fat 2 g, Monounsaturated Fat 8 g, Polyunsaturated Fat 1 g, Cholesterol 24 mg, Sodium 745 mg, Fiber 10 g

Turkey Meat Loaf

Delores A. Gnagey, Saginaw, MI
Makes 10 servings

Prep. Time: 20 minutes   ⚘   Baking Time: 90 minutes   ⚘   Standing Time: 10 minutes

2 lbs. skinless, dark and white turkey meat, ground

Half a medium onion (½ cup), minced

3 Tbsp. minced fresh parsley

2 egg whites, or egg substitute equivalent to 1 egg

¼ cup skim milk

1 tsp. dry mustard

¼ tsp. salt

¼ tsp. ground white pepper

⅛ tsp. nutmeg

2 slices whole wheat bread, lightly toasted, made into coarse crumbs

2 Tbsp. ketchup

2 Tbsp. water

1. Preheat oven to 350°.

2. Mix together ground turkey, onion, and parsley in a large bowl. Set aside.

3. In a medium bowl, whisk egg whites, or egg substitute, until frothy.

4. Add milk, mustard, salt, pepper, and nutmeg to egg. Whisk to blend.

5. Add bread crumbs to egg mixture. Let rest 10 minutes.

6. Add egg mixture to meat mixture and blend well.

7. Shape into loaf. Place in 5 × 9 loaf pan.

8. Blend together ketchup and water in a small bowl. Spread mixture on top of meat.

9. Bake until meat is no longer pink, about 90 minutes.

10. Allow meat to stand 10 minutes before slicing to serve.

Per Serving

Calories 173, Kilojoules 724, Protein 18 g, Carbohydrates 7 g, Total Fat 8 g, Saturated Fat 2 g, Monounsaturated Fat 4 g, Polyunsaturated Fat 2 g, Cholesterol 72 mg, Sodium 223 mg, Fiber 1 g

Pork

Brown Sugar Pork Chops

Andrea Maher, Dunedin, FL
Makes 6 servings

Prep. Time: 5 minutes ☙ *Cooking Time: 6–8 hours* ☙ *Ideal slow cooker size: 5- or 6-qt.*

2 Tbsp. garlic powder

2 tsp. Dijon mustard

3 Tbsp. apple cider vinegar

¼ teaspoon pepper

¼ teaspoon kosher salt

⅓ cup water

¼ cup brown sugar or ¼ cup sugar-free maple syrup

3 cups pineapple slices

24 oz. pork chops

½ cup chopped celery

1. Combine all ingredients in slow cooker.

2. Cover and cook on high for 3–4 hours or on low for 6–8 hours.

Per Serving

Calories 218, Kilojoules 913, Protein 26 g, Carbohydrates 19 g, Total Fat 4 g, Saturated Fat 1 g, Monounsaturated Fat 1.5 g, Polyunsaturated Fat 0.5 g, Cholesterol 80 mg, Sodium 200 mg, Fiber 2 g

Carnitas

SLOW COOKER

Hope Comerford, Clinton Township, MI
Makes 12 servings

Prep. Time: 10 minutes ⚹ *Cooking Time: 10–12 hours* ⚹ *Ideal slow cooker size: 4-qt.*

2 lb. pork shoulder roast

1 ½ tsp. kosher salt

½ tsp. pepper

2 tsp. cumin

5 cloves garlic, minced

1 tsp. oregano

3 bay leaves

2 cups gluten-free chicken stock

2 Tbsp. lime juice

1 tsp. lime zest

12 6" gluten-free white corn tortillas

1. Place pork shoulder roast in crock.

2. Mix together the salt, pepper, cumin, garlic, and oregano. Rub it onto the pork roast.

3. Place the bay leaves around the pork roast, then pour in the chicken stock around the roast, being careful not to wash off the spices.

4. Cover and cook on low for 10–12 hours.

5. Remove the roast with a slotted spoon, as well as the bay leaves. Shred the pork between 2 forks, then replace the shredded pork in the crock and stir.

6. Add the lime juice and lime zest to the crock and stir.

7. Serve on warmed white corn tortillas.

Per Serving
Calories 63, Kilojoules 262, Protein 17 g,
Carbohydrates 12 g, Total Fat 5 g, Saturated Fat 2 g,
Monounsaturated Fat 2 g, Polyunsaturated Fat 0.7 g,
Cholesterol 0 mg, Sodium 330 mg, Fiber 2 g

Healthy Sloppy Joes

Gladys M. High, Ephrata, PA
Makes 4 servings

Prep. Time: 20 minutes 🞕 Cooking Time: 20 minutes

¾ lb. 90%-lean ground pork loin

1 cup chopped onion

1 medium bell sweet pepper, chopped

1½ cups diced tomatoes, no salt added, undrained

1 medium zucchini, shredded, optional

1 Tbsp. chili powder

1 tsp. paprika

½ tsp. minced garlic

Pepper to taste

3 Tbsp. tomato paste

4 whole wheat hamburger buns

1. In large skillet, cook ground pork, onion, and bell pepper until meat is brown and onion is tender. Drain off drippings.

2. Stir in diced tomatoes, zucchini if you wish, chili powder, paprika, garlic, and pepper. Cover and bring to a boil. Reduce heat.

3. Add tomato paste to thicken. Simmer, uncovered, for 5 minutes.

4. Spoon mixture into buns and enjoy.

Per Serving

Calories 343, Kilojoules 1435, Protein 27 g, Carbohydrates 44 g, Total Fat 7 g, Saturated Fat 2 g, Monounsaturated Fat 3.5 g, Polyunsaturated Fat 1.5 g, Cholesterol 53 mg, Sodium 273 mg, Fiber 7 g

Pork Kabobs in Pita Bread

Susan Kasting, Jenks, OK
Makes 8 servings

Prep. Time: 20 minutes ⚜ *Marinating Time: 8 hours or overnight* ⚜ *Grilling Time: 8–10 minutes*

Marinade:

2 lb. boneless pork loin, cut into 1" cubes

¼ cup vegetable oil

¼ cup chopped onion

3 Tbsp. lemon juice

1 Tbsp. chopped parsley

1 clove garlic, minced

½ tsp. dried marjoram

⅛ tsp. pepper

Sauce:

1 cup plain fat-free yogurt

½ cup chopped cucumber

1 Tbsp. chopped onion

1 Tbsp. chopped parsley

1 clove garlic, minced

1 tsp. lemon juice

8 whole wheat pita bread rounds

1. Mix marinade and pork in a re-sealable plastic bag.

2. Place bag with meat and marinade in a bowl (in case of leaks). Refrigerate overnight.

3. Mix sauce ingredients in a bowl.

4. Drain pork. Place on skewers or on a grill pan.

5. Grill 8–10 minutes, turning over at least once.

6. Serve pork in pita bread topped with sauce.

Tip:

Heat pitas to make them pliable.

Per Serving

Calories 301, Kilojoules 1259, Protein 33 g, Carbohydrates 33 g, Total Fat 5 g, Saturated Fat 1 g, Monounsaturated Fat 1.5 g, Polyunsaturated Fat 2.5 g, Cholesterol 74 mg, Sodium 428 mg, Fiber 6 g

Beef

Low-Fat Slow Cooker Roast

SLOW COOKER

Charlotte Shaffer, East Earl, PA
Makes 10 servings

Prep. Time: 15 minutes ⚘ *Cooking Time: 3–8 hours* ⚘ *Ideal slow cooker size: 6-qt.*

3 lb. boneless beef roast

4 carrots, peeled and cut into 2" pieces

4 potatoes, cut into quarters

2 onions, quartered

1 cup gluten-free, low-sodium beef broth or stock

1 tsp. garlic powder

1 tsp. Mrs. Dash seasoning

½ tsp. salt

½ tsp. black pepper

1. Place roast in slow cooker.

2. Add carrots around edges, pushing them down so they reach the bottom of the crock.

3. Add potatoes and onions.

4. Mix together broth and seasonings and pour over roast.

5. Cover and cook on low for 6–8 hours, or on high for 3–4 hours.

Per Serving

Calories 273, Kilojoules 1145, Protein 31 g, Carbohydrates 19 g, Total Fat 9 g, Saturated Fat 3 g, Monounsaturated Fat 3.5 g, Polyunsaturated Fat 0.6 g, Cholesterol 75 mg, Sodium 230 mg, Fiber 2.5 g

Herb Marinated Steak

Linda E. Wilcox, Blythewood, SC
Makes 4 servings

Prep. Time: 10 minutes ⚜ *Marinating Time: 6–8 hours* ⚜
Cooking/Baking Time: 12–18 minutes ⚜ *Standing Time: 10 minutes*

¼ cup chopped onion
2 Tbsp. fresh parsley
2 Tbsp. balsamic vinegar
1 Tbsp. olive oil
2 tsp. Dijon-style mustard
1 clove garlic minced
1 lb. London broil, or chuck steak

1. Combine onion, parsley, vinegar, oil, mustard, and garlic in a bowl.

2. Place London broil or chuck steak in a sturdy plastic bag. Add onion mixture, spreading it on both sides of the meat. Close bag securely.

3. Place filled bag in a long dish in case of any leaks. Marinate in refrigerator 6–8 hours, or overnight. Turn it over at least once while marinating.

4. Pour off marinade. Place steak on rack in broiler pan so meat is about 5″ from heat source. Broil about 6–8 minutes on each side for rare; 9 minutes on each side for medium.

5. When finished broiling, allow meat to stand for 10 minutes.

6. Then carve diagonally across the grain into thin slices.

Tip:
You can grill the steak, rather than broiling it.

Per Serving
Calories 210, Kilojoules 879, Protein 23 g,
Carbohydrates 4 g, Total Fat 10 g, Saturated Fat 3 g,
Monounsaturated Fat 6 g, Polyunsaturated Fat 1 g,
Cholesterol 64 mg, Sodium 132 mg, Fiber trace

Four Pepper Steak

SLOW COOKER

Renee Hankins, Narvon, PA
Makes 14 servings

Prep. Time: 30 minutes ⚘ *Cooking Time: 5–8 hours* ⚘ *Ideal slow cooker size: 4- or 5-qt.*

1 yellow pepper, sliced into ¼" thick pieces

1 red pepper, sliced into ¼" thick pieces

1 orange pepper, sliced into ¼"thick pieces

1 green pepper, sliced into ¼" thick pieces

2 garlic cloves, sliced

2 large onions, sliced

1 tsp. ground cumin

½ tsp. dried oregano

1 bay leaf

3 lb. flank steak, cut in ¼–½" thick slices across the grain

Salt to taste

2 14½ -oz. cans low-sodium diced tomatoes in juice

Jalapeño chilies, sliced, optional

1. Place sliced bell peppers, garlic, onions, cumin, oregano, and bay leaf in slow cooker. Stir gently to mix.

2. Put steak slices on top of vegetable mixture. Season with salt.

3. Spoon tomatoes with juice over top. Sprinkle with jalapeño pepper slices if you wish. Do not stir.

4. Cover and cook on low 5–8 hours, depending on your slow cooker. Check after 5 hours to see if meat is tender. If not, continue cooking until tender but not dry. Remove bay leaf and serve.

Per Serving
Calories 191, Kilojoules 799, Protein 22 g, Carbohydrates 7 g, Total Fat 8 g, Saturated Fat 3 g, Monounsaturated Fat 4 g, Polyunsaturated Fat 0.4 g, Cholesterol 45 mg, Sodium 160 mg, Fiber 1 g

Zesty Pasta

Carol Collins, Holly Springs, NC
Makes 8 servings

Prep. Time: 10 minutes   ❧   *Cooking Time: 1¾–2¼ hours*

½ Tbsp. olive oil

1½ cups chopped onion

1 lb. 95%-lean ground sirloin, or bison

3 garlic cloves, minced

2 tsp. black pepper

1 tsp. dried oregano

28-oz. can tomato puree, no salt added

15-oz. can tomato sauce, no salt added

½ tsp. sugar, optional

1 lb. uncooked whole wheat pasta

1. Heat olive oil in large stockpot over medium heat. Add onions and sauté until golden. Remove onions with slotted spoon and reserve.

2. Add ground meat and garlic to stockpot. Cook until meat is browned and no longer pink inside.

3. Add reserved onions, black pepper, oregano, tomato puree, and tomato sauce. Cook over low heat, partially covered, for 1½ hours.

4. Stir occasionally. Add water by ¼ cupfuls if sauce appears too thick.

5. Adjust taste with sugar if you wish.

6. Cook pasta according to package directions. Drain and top with pasta sauce.

Tips:

1. If preparing this recipe for young children, reduce black pepper to 1 tsp.

2. Serve this sauce over hearty pasta like thick spaghetti or cavatappi (spiral hollow noodles).

3. Use leftover sauce as a topping for pizza.

Per Serving (optional sugar not included in analysis)
Calories 381, Kilojoules 1594, Protein 22 g,
Carbohydrates 62 g, Total Fat 5 g, Saturated Fat 1.5 g,
Monounsaturated Fat 2 g, Polyunsaturated Fat 1 g,
Cholesterol 35 mg, Sodium 90 mg, Fiber 10 g

Zucchini Lasagna

Carolyn Snader, Ephrata, PA
Makes 6 servings

Prep. Time: 15–20 minutes ⚜ Cooking/Baking Time: 30–35 minutes

6 cups sliced, unpeeled, zucchini

1 lb. 95%-lean ground beef

½ tsp. dried basil

½ tsp. dried oregano

⅛ tsp. garlic powder

6-oz. can tomato paste, no salt added

1 cup low-fat cottage cheese

Egg substitute equivalent to 1 egg, or 2 egg whites

2 cups shredded low-fat mozzarella cheese, divided

1. Cook sliced zucchini 7–10 minutes on High in microwave, if you wish.

2. Brown ground beef in a skillet.

3. Add basil, oregano, and garlic powder to the beef.

4. Add tomato paste to meat and stir together.

5. In a bowl, mix cottage cheese, egg, and 1 cup mozzarella cheese together.

6. In a lightly greased 9 × 13 baking dish, layer in half the zucchini, half the meat with seasonings, and half the cottage cheese mixture.

7. Repeat layers.

8. Top with remaining cup of mozzarella cheese.

9. Bake, uncovered, at 350° for 30–35 minutes.

Per Serving

Calories 274, Kilojoules 1146, Protein 32 g, Carbohydrates 12 g, Total Fat 11 g, Saturated Fat 6 g, Monounsaturated Fat 4 g, Polyunsaturated Fat 1 g, Cholesterol 71 mg, Sodium 368 mg, Fiber 2.5 g

Stuffed Cabbage

Becky Gehman, Bergton, VA
Makes 6 servings

Prep. Time: 15–20 minutes & Cooking Time: 1 hour, 40 minutes

6–7 large cabbage leaves

1 lb. 95%-fat-free hamburger, or extra-lean turkey burger

1 tsp. diced fine onion

¼ tsp. salt

½ tsp. pepper

3 Tbsp. brown rice, uncooked

1 can low-sodium tomato soup

1 soup can water

1 tsp. Italian seasoning without salt, such as Mrs. Dash, optional

1 Tbsp. vinegar

1. Place cabbage leaves in large stockpot. Cover with water. Cover pot and cook cabbage until just tender. Remove leaves from water and drain.

2. Mix hamburger or turkey burger, onion, salt, pepper, and rice together in a bowl.

3. Divide this mixture among the 6 or 7 cooked cabbage leaves. Place in the middle of each leaf.

4. Wrap cabbage leaves around meat mixture to make 6 bundles. Secure each with 2 toothpicks to keep them from unwrapping.

5. Heat tomato soup, water, and Italian seasoning if you wish, in a large saucepan.

6. Carefully lay cabbage bundles in tomato soup mixture.

7. Allow to simmer, covered, 1½ hours.

8. Stir in vinegar 10 minutes before end of cooking time.

Per Serving

Calories 172, Kilojoules 720, Protein 18 g, Carbohydrates 13 g, Total Fat 5 g, Saturated Fat 2 g, Monounsaturated Fat 1.5 g, Polyunsaturated Fat 1.5 g, Cholesterol 47 mg, Sodium 174 mg, Fiber 2 g

Seafood

Cajun Catfish

SLOW COOKER

Hope Comerford, Clinton Township, MI
Makes 4 servings

Prep. Time: 5 minutes ⚬ *Cooking Time: 2 hours* ⚬ *Ideal slow cooker size: 6-qt.*

4–6 oz. catfish filets
2 tsp. paprika
1 tsp. black pepper
1 tsp. oregano
1 tsp. dried thyme
½ tsp. garlic powder
½ tsp. kosher salt
½ tsp. parsley flakes
¼ tsp. cayenne pepper
1 Tbsp. coconut oil

1. Pat the catfish filets dry.

2. Mix together the paprika, black pepper, oregano, thyme, garlic powder, salt, parsley flakes, and cayenne.

3. Place parchment paper in your crock and push it down so it forms against the inside of the crock. Place the coconut oil in the crock.

4. Coat each side of the catfish filet with the spice mixture, then place them in the crock.

5. Cover and cook on low for about 2 hours, or until the fish flakes easily with a fork.

Per Serving

Calories 240, Kilojoules 1004, Protein 26 g, Carbohydrates 2 g, Total Fat 14 g, Saturated Fat 5 g, Monounsaturated Fat 4.6 g, Polyunsaturated Fat 2 g, Cholesterol 94 mg, Sodium 287 mg, Fiber 1 g

Maple-Glazed Salmon

Jenelle Miller, Marion, SD
Makes 6 servings

Prep. Time: 10 minutes & *Grilling Time: 8–9 minutes*

2 tsp. paprika
2 tsp. chili powder
½ tsp. ground cumin
½ tsp. brown sugar
1 tsp. kosher salt, optional
6 4-oz. salmon fillets
1 Tbsp. maple syrup

1. Spray grill rack with cooking spray. Heat grill to medium.

2. Combine first four ingredients in a small bowl.

3. Sprinkle fillets with salt if you wish. Rub with paprika mixture.

4. Place fish on grill rack. Grill 7 minutes.

5. Drizzle fish with maple syrup.

6. Grill 1–2 minutes more, or until fish flakes easily when tested with a fork.

Per Serving (optional salt is not included in analysis)

Calories 221, Kilojoules 925, Protein 23 g,
Carbohydrates 3 g, Total Fat 13 g, Saturated Fat 3 g,
Monounsaturated Fat 5 g, Polyunsaturated Fat 5 g,
Cholesterol 66 mg, Sodium 397 mg, Fiber 0.5 g

Quick Salmon Patties

Dorothy VanDeest, Memphis, TN
Makes 3 servings

Prep. Time: 10 minutes ⚓ *Cooking Time: 3–4 minutes*

2 6-oz. cans salmon, boned, skinned, and drained

2 egg whites, or egg substitute equivalent to 1 egg

½ tsp. Worcestershire sauce

⅛ tsp. pepper

⅓ cup finely chopped onion

5 soda crackers with unsalted tops, crushed

2 tsp. olive oil

1. In a good-sized bowl, combine first six ingredients and mix well.

2. Shape into six patties.

3. In a skillet, cook patties in oil over medium heat for 1½–2 minutes.

4. Flip patties over. Cook 1½–2 minutes more, or until heated through.

Per Serving

Calories 220, Kilojoules 920, Protein 29 g, Carbohydrates 5 g, Total Fat 9 g, Saturated Fat 1.5 g, Monounsaturated Fat 5 g, Polyunsaturated Fat 2.5 g, Cholesterol 92 mg, Sodium 537 mg, Fiber 0.5 g

Thai Shrimp and Rice

Pat Bechtel, Dillsburg, PA
Makes 6 servings

Prep. Time: 10 minutes ❧ *Cooking Time: 25–30 minutes*

1 tsp. olive oil

½ cup sliced scallions

1 Tbsp. chopped garlic

14-oz. can light coconut milk water

1½ cups jasmine, or converted, white rice

1 cup shredded carrots

1 tsp. salt

12 oz. raw shrimp, peeled and deveined

2½ cups (about ½ lb.) fresh snow peas

2 tsp. lime zest

Lime wedges

Cilantro for garnish

1. Heat olive oil in a large skillet over medium heat. Sauté scallions and garlic.

2. Pour coconut milk into a quart measure. Add enough water to make 3¼ cups.

3. Add milk mixture to skillet and bring to a boil.

4. Stir in rice, carrots, and salt.

5. Cover. Reduce heat and simmer 12 minutes, or until rice is nearly tender.

6. Stir in shrimp, snow peas, and lime zest. If rice looks dry add ¼ cup water.

7. Cover and bring to a simmer. Cook 3–4 minutes, or until shrimp and peas are crisp-tender.

8. Garnish with lime wedges and chopped cilantro just before serving.

Tip:
Cook shrimp only until pink.

Per Serving

Calories 296, Kilojoules 1238, Protein 17 g, Carbohydrates 44 g, Total Fat 6 g, Saturated Fat 4 g, Monounsaturated Fat 1 g, Polyunsaturated Fat 1 g, Cholesterol 86 mg, Sodium 499 mg, Fiber 4 g

Shrimp Stir-Fry

Jean Binns Smith, Bellefonte, PA
Makes 4 servings

Prep. Time: 10 minutes ⚘ *Cooking Time: 8–10 minutes*

1–2 cloves garlic, chopped

⅛ tsp. grated, or finely chopped, fresh ginger

1 Tbsp. olive oil

2½ cups (about ½ lb.) fresh sugar snap peas

½ cup chopped red bell sweet pepper, optional

12 oz. medium-sized raw shrimp, peeled and deveined

1. Sauté garlic and ginger in oil in large skillet until fragrant.

2. Stir in sugar peas and chopped pepper if you wish. Sauté until crisp-tender.

3. Stir in shrimp. Cook over medium heat 3–4 minutes until shrimp are just opaque in centers.

Serving suggestion:

Serve with steamed rice (not included in analyses).

Per Serving

Calories 156, Kilojoules 653, Protein 19 g,
Carbohydrates 8 g, Total Fat 5 g, Saturated Fat 0.7 g,
Monounsaturated Fat 2.5 g, Polyunsaturated Fat 1.8 g,
Cholesterol 129 mg, Sodium 136 mg, Fiber 2 g

Meatless

Pasta Primavera

Marcia S. Myer, Manheim, PA
Makes 6 main-dish servings

Prep. Time: 20–30 minutes ⚘ *Cooking Time: 25 minutes*

3 cups broccoli florets, cut bite-size

½ lb. fresh mushrooms, quartered

2 small zucchini, sliced into ¼"-thick rounds

1 Tbsp. olive oil

1–3 cloves garlic, minced, according to your taste preference

1 pint cherry tomatoes, halved

8-oz. pkg. whole-grain fettuccine

Black pepper to taste

3 Tbsp. grated reduced-fat Parmesan cheese

Sauce:

¾ cup skim milk

1 Tbsp. olive oil

⅔ cup part-skim ricotta cheese

¼ cup grated reduced-fat Parmesan cheese

2 Tbsp. chopped fresh basil, or 1 Tbsp. dried basil

2 tsp. dry sherry

1. In large microwave-safe bowl, layer in broccoli, mushrooms, and zucchini. Cover bowl and microwave on high for 2 minutes.

2. Stir. Cover and cook another 2 minutes on high, or until tender-crisp.

3. In non-stick skillet, heat olive oil. Add garlic and sauté for 1 minute. Add tomatoes and sauté for 2 minutes, or until tomatoes are slightly cooked but not wilted.

4. Cook fettuccine as directed with no salt. Drain. Keep warm.

5. Prepare sauce by combining milk, oil, ricotta cheese, Parmesan cheese, basil, and sherry in a blender.

6. Process until smooth. Heat sauce until warm, on stove or in microwave.

7. In large serving bowl, toss drained pasta, vegetables, and sauce.

8. Garnish with black pepper.

Per Serving

Calories 283, Kilojoules 1184, Protein 13 g, Carbohydrates 40 g, Total Fat 8 g, Saturated Fat 2 g, Monounsaturated Fat 4 g, Polyunsaturated Fat 2 g, Cholesterol 12 mg, Sodium 159 mg, Fiber 7 g

Faked You Out Alfredo

SLOW COOKER

Sue Hamilton, Benson, AZ
Makes 4 servings

Prep. Time: 5 minutes   Cooking Time: 6 hours   Ideal slow cooker size: 3-qt.

1 lb. bag of frozen cauliflower

1 13½-oz. can light coconut milk

½ cup diced onion

2 cloves garlic, minced

1 Tbsp. vegetable stock concentrate

Salt and pepper to taste

1. Place the frozen cauliflower, coconut milk, onion, garlic, and the vegetable stock concentrate in your crock. Stir mixture to blend in the stock concentrate.

2. Cover and cook on low for 6 hours.

3. Place cooked mixture in blender and process until smooth.

4. Add salt and pepper to taste.

Serving suggestion:

Serve over cooked pasta, cooked sliced potatoes, or any other vegetable.

Tip:

My husband loves this on pasta with cooked mushrooms mixed in. This sauce can be made ahead of time and refrigerated.

Per Serving

Calories 92, Kilojoules 385, Protein 3 g, Carbohydrates 7 g, Total Fat 6 g, Saturated Fat 5 g, Monounsaturated Fat 0 g, Polyunsaturated Fat 0 g, Cholesterol 0 mg, Sodium 664 mg, Fiber 1 g

Fresh Veggie Lasagna

SLOW COOKER

Deanne Gingrich, Lancaster, PA
Makes 4–6 servings

Prep. Time: 30 minutes ❧ *Cooking Time: 4 hours* ❧ *Ideal slow cooker size: 4- or 5-qt.*

1½ cups shredded low-fat mozzarella cheese

½ cup low-fat ricotta cheese

⅓ cup grated Parmesan cheese

1 egg, lightly beaten

1 tsp. dried oregano

¼ tsp. garlic powder

3 cups marinara sauce, divided

1 medium zucchini, diced, divided

4 uncooked gluten-free lasagna noodles

4 cups fresh baby spinach, divided

1 cup fresh mushrooms, sliced, divided

1. Grease interior of slow cooker crock.

2. In a bowl, mix together mozzarella, ricotta, and Parmesan cheeses, egg, oregano, and garlic powder. Set aside.

3. Spread ½ cup marinara sauce in crock.

4. Sprinkle with half the zucchini.

5. Spoon ⅓ of cheese mixture over zucchini.

6. Break 2 noodles into large pieces to cover cheese layer.

7. Spread ½ cup marinara over noodles.

8. Top with half the spinach and then half the mushrooms.

9. Repeat layers, ending with cheese mixture, and then sauce. Press layers down firmly.

10. Cover and cook on low for 4 hours, or until vegetables are as tender as you like them and noodles are fully cooked.

11. Let stand 15 minutes so lasagna can firm up before serving.

Per Serving

Calories 242, Kilojoules 1013, Protein 15 g, Carbohydrates 22 g, Total Fat 10 g, Saturated Fat 5 g, Monounsaturated Fat 2 g, Polyunsaturated Fat 0.5 g, Cholesterol 59 mg, Sodium 763 mg, Fiber 3 g

Eggplant Parmesan

Mary Ann Bowman, East Earl, PA
Makes 6 main-dish servings

Prep. Time: 15 minutes & *Broiling/Baking Time: 40–45 minutes*

1 medium eggplant, unpeeled
2 Tbsp. olive oil, divided
1 cup bread crumbs
½ tsp. dried basil
½ cup grated Parmesan cheese
2 Tbsp. chopped parsley
⅛ tsp. pepper
1 tsp. dried oregano
6 tomatoes, chopped
2 green bell sweet peppers, chopped
2 onions, chopped
1 clove garlic, chopped
2 Tbsp. tomato paste
1 cup grated Swiss cheese
¼ cup additional Parmesan cheese

Per Serving

Calories 309, Kilojoules 1293,
Protein 15 g,
Carbohydrates 30 g, Total Fat 15 g,
Saturated Fat 6 g,
Monounsaturated Fat 6 g,
Polyunsaturated Fat 3 g,
Cholesterol 29 mg, Sodium 343
mg, Fiber 7 g

1. Preheat oven to broil.

2. Cut eggplant into 6 slices, each ½" thick.

3. Place slices on cookie sheet. Brush with half the olive oil.

4. Broil 5 minutes, or until golden.

5. Turn slices. Brush other sides with remaining oil.

6. Return to broiler and brown second sides.

7. Place browned eggplant in lightly greased 9 × 13 baking pan, sprayed generously with non-stick cooking spray.

8. Mix together next 6 ingredients in a small bowl. Sprinkle over eggplant.

9. Combine in saucepan tomatoes, peppers, onions, garlic, and tomato paste. Simmer uncovered about 20 minutes.

10. Then spread on top of crumb mixture.

11. Top with Swiss cheese and additional Parmesan cheese.

12. Bake uncovered at 375° for 10–15 minutes.

Tip:
You can make this ahead and refrigerate it until you're ready to heat and serve it.

Spicy Mexican Bean Burgers

Lois Hess, Lancaster, PA
Makes 4 burgers

Prep. Time: 30 minutes ❧ Baking Time: 15–20 minutes

16-oz. can red kidney beans, rinsed, drained, and mashed

½ cup onion, chopped

Half a green bell sweet pepper, chopped

1 carrot, steamed and mashed

⅛ cup salsa, your choice of flavors

1 cup whole wheat bread crumbs

½ cup whole wheat flour

½ tsp. black pepper, optional

Dash of chili powder

1. Heat oven to 400°.

2. Combine all ingredients in a good-sized bowl. Add more flour to create a firmer mixture or more salsa if mixture is too stiff.

3. Form into 4 balls and then flatten into patties.

4. Place on a baking sheet, lightly sprayed with cooking spray.

5. Bake 15–20 minutes, or until firm and brown.

Serving Suggestion:

Serve on a whole wheat bun with lettuce, tomato, and salsa. (These ingredients are not included in the nutritional analyses.)

Per Serving
Calories 123, Kilojoules 515, Protein 5 g,
Carbohydrates 23 g, Total Fat 1 g, Saturated Fat 0.2 g,
Monounsaturated Fat 0.6 g, Polyunsaturated Fat 0.2 g,
Cholesterol trace, Sodium 200 mg, Fiber 5 g

Black Bean Lasagna Rolls

Janelle Reitz, Lancaster, PA
Makes 8 main-dish servings

Prep. Time: 15 minutes   Cooking/Baking Time: 40 minutes

1 cup shredded reduced-fat Monterey Jack cheese

1 cup low-fat cottage cheese

4½-oz. can chopped green chilies, rinsed and drained

½ tsp. chili powder

8 whole-grain lasagna noodles, uncooked

2 cups cooked black beans, rinsed and drained

15½-oz. jar salsa

1. Combine first 4 ingredients in a bowl, stirring well.

2. Cook lasagna noodles according to package directions, omitting salt and fat. Drain well. Rinse to keep noodles from sticking together.

3. Spread a portion of cheese mixture over each noodle. Spoon black beans evenly over cheese mixture.

4. Lightly grease a 7 × 11 baking dish. Roll up noodles, jelly-roll fashion, beginning at narrow end. Place lasagna rolls, seam-side down, in baking dish.

5. Pour salsa over rolls.

6. Cover and bake at 350° for 25 minutes, or until thoroughly heated.

Per Serving

Calories 214, Kilojoules 895, Protein 13 g,
Carbohydrates 33 g, Total Fat 4 g, Saturated Fat 2 g,
Monounsaturated Fat 1 g, Polyunsaturated Fat 1 g,
Cholesterol 11 mg, Sodium 786 mg, Fiber 5 g

Vegetables and Side Dishes

Holiday Green Beans

Joanne Kennedy, Plattsburgh, NY
Jean Ryan, Peru, NY
Makes 10 servings

Prep. Time: 10 minutes ⚬ *Cooking Time: 20–30 minutes*

2 lb. (about 8 cups) fresh green beans
1 large red onion, thinly sliced
3 cloves fresh garlic, minced
1 tsp. olive oil
½ cup slivered almonds
Pepper to taste

1. Steam beans in saucepan until just slightly crisp.

2. Sauté onion and garlic in olive oil in large skillet for 3 minutes.

3. Add beans to skillet. Sauté 1 minute.

4. Add slivered almonds and pepper to beans. Toss together and then serve.

Per Serving
Calories 73, Kilojoules 305, Protein 3 g,
Carbohydrates 7 g, Total Fat 4 g, Saturated Fat 0.3 g,
Monounsaturated Fat 2.2 g, Polyunsaturated Fat 1.5 g,
Cholesterol 0 mg, Sodium 6 mg, Fiber 4 g

Zucchini Ribbons

Delores Gnagey, Saginaw, MI
Makes 4 servings

Prep. Time: 15 minutes 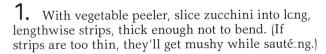 Cooking Time: 9 minutes

1 large zucchini, unpeeled, ends
trimmed

1 Tbsp. olive oil

3 garlic cloves, minced

1 cup cherry tomato halves

1 tsp. fresh basil, finely chopped

Pepper to taste

1. With vegetable peeler, slice zucchini into long, lengthwise strips, thick enough not to bend. (If strips are too thin, they'll get mushy while sautéing.)

2. Heat oil in large skillet over medium heat. Add zucchini ribbons. Sauté 4 minutes.

3. Add garlic and sauté 2 more minutes.

4. Add cherry tomatoes and sauté 2 additional minutes.

5. Sprinkle with basil and pepper to taste. Cook 1 minute.

Per Serving

Calories 58, Kilojoules 243, Protein 1 g,
Carbohydrates 5 g, Total Fat 4 g, Saturated Fat 0.5 g,
Monounsaturated Fat 2.5 g, Polyunsaturated Fat 1 g,
Cholesterol 0 mg, Sodium 13 mg, Fiber 2 g

Broccoli Salad

Mary Seielstad, Sparks, NV
Makes 6 servings

Prep. Time: 15 minutes ❧ *Chilling Time: 8 hours, or overnight*

Dressing:

½ cup light, or reduced-fat, mayonnaise

2 Tbsp. sugar

2 tsp. red wine vinegar

Salad:

1 medium head broccoli, cut into florets (about 3 cups)

1 red bell sweet pepper, chopped

4 green onions, chopped

¼ cup chopped walnuts

1. Combine dressing ingredients in a jar with a tight-fitting lid. Shake to combine and chill overnight.

2. Combine salad ingredients. Pour dressing over salad and toss to mix.

Per Serving

Calories 88, Kilojoules 368, Protein 3 g,
Carbohydrates 10 g, Total Fat 4 g, Saturated Fat 0.5 g,
Monounsaturated Fat 1.5 g, Polyunsaturated Fat 2 g,
Cholesterol 0 mg, Sodium 178 mg, Fiber 3 g

Honey-Glazed Carrots

Janet Oberholtzer, Ephrata, PA
Makes 4 servings

Prep. Time: 5 minutes ⚮ *Cooking Time: 10–15 minutes*

6 medium carrots, peeled and chopped into 2" chunks

2 tsp. olive oil

1 Tbsp. honey

½ Tbsp. fresh lemon juice

1. Cook carrots in a bit of water in a saucepan until they're as tender as you like.

2. Meanwhile, combine olive oil, honey, and lemon juice in a small microwave-safe dish. Microwave on high 20–30 seconds. Stir.

3. Drain carrots. Pour glaze over top and toss to coat.

Per Serving

Calories 76, Kilojoules 318, Protein 1 g, Carbohydrates 13 g, Total Fat 2.5 g, Saturated Fat 0.3 g, Monounsaturated Fat 1.7 g, Polyunsaturated Fat 0.5 g, Cholesterol 0 mg, Sodium 89 mg, Fiber 3 g

Roasted Broccoli

Andrea Cunningham, Arlington, KS
Makes 4 servings

Prep. Time: 10 minutes ⚬ *Baking Time: 20 minutes*

1 head (about 5 cups) broccoli, cut into long pieces all the way through (you will eat the stems)

1 Tbsp. olive oil

2–3 cloves garlic, sliced thin

Pepper

Lemon wedges

1. Preheat oven to 400°.

2. Place broccoli in baking pan with sides. Drizzle with olive oil. Toss to coat.

3. Sprinkle garlic and pepper over top.

4. Transfer to oven and roast 15–20 minutes, or until broccoli is crispy on the ends and a little browned.

5. Sprinkle with lemon juice.

Per Serving

Calories 71, Kilojoules 297, Protein 3 g, Carbohydrates 6 g, Total Fat 4 g, Saturated Fat 0.5 g, Monounsaturated Fat 2.5 g, Polyunsaturated Fat 1 g, Cholesterol 0 mg, Sodium 38 mg, Fiber 3 g

Cauliflower Mashed "Potatoes"

Anne Hummel, Millersburg, OH
Makes 4 servings

Prep. Time: 20 minutes ⚬ Cooking Time: 20–30 minutes

I head cauliflower

I clove garlic

I leek, white only, split in 4 pieces

I Tbsp. soft-tub margarine, non-hydrogenated

Pepper to taste

1. Break cauliflower into small pieces.

2. In a good-sized saucepan, steam cauliflower, garlic, and leek in water until completely tender, about 20–30 minutes.

3. While cauliflower is hot, puree until the vegetables resemble mashed potatoes. (Use a food processor, or if you prefer a smoother texture, use a blender. Process only a small portion at a time, holding the blender lid on firmly with a tea towel.)

4. Add a little hot water if vegetables seem dry.

5. Stir in margarine and pepper to taste.

Per Serving

Calories 67, Kilojoules 280, Protein 2 g,
Carbohydrates 9 g, Total Fat 3 g, Saturated Fat 0.5 g,
Monounsaturated Fat 1.5 g, Polyunsaturated Fat 1 g,
Cholesterol 0 mg, Sodium 75 mg, Fiber 3 g

Orange-Glazed Carrots

SLOW COOKER

Cyndie Marrara, Port Matilda, PA
Makes 6 servings

Prep. Time: 5–10 minutes ⚜ *Cooking Time: 3–4 hours* ⚜ *Ideal slow cooker size: 3½-qt.*

32-oz. (2 lb.) pkg. baby carrots

⅓ cup turbinado sugar

2–3 oranges, squeezed for juice to make approx. ½ cup juice

3 Tbsp. coconut oil, melted

¾ tsp. cinnamon

¼ tsp. nutmeg

2 Tbsp. cornstarch

¼ cup water

1. Combine all ingredients except cornstarch and water in slow cooker.

2. Cover. Cook on low 3–4 hours, until carrots are tender crisp.

3. Put carrots in serving dish and keep warm reserving cooking juices. Put reserved juices in small saucepan. Bring to boil.

4. Mix cornstarch and water in small bowl until blended. Add to juices. Boil one minute or until thickened, stirring constantly.

5. Pour over carrots and serve.

Serving suggestion:

Sprinkle with orange zest before serving.

Per Serving
Calories 204, Kilojoules 855, Protein 2 g,
Carbohydrates 35 g, Total Fat 7 g, Saturated Fat 6 g,
Monounsaturated Fat 0.5 g, Polyunsaturated Fat 0.3 g,
Cholesterol 0 mg, Sodium 105 mg, Fiber 6 g

Baked Corn

Samuel Stoltzfus, Bird-in-Hand, PA
Makes 8 servings

Prep. Time: 15 minutes ♣ *Baking Time: 35–50 minutes*

2 cups corn

2 eggs, slightly beaten, or 4 egg whites, slightly beaten

1 tsp. sugar

1 Tbsp. soft-tub margarine, melted

2 Tbsp. flour

1 cup skim milk

¼ tsp. salt

1. Mix all ingredients together in a large bowl.

2. Pour into a greased 2-quart baking dish.

3. Bake at 350° for 35–50 minutes, or until corn is firm in the middle and browned around the edges.

Per Serving

Calories 73, Kilojoules 305, Protein 4 g,
Carbohydrates 11 g, Total Fat 2 g, Saturated Fat 0.4 g,
Monounsaturated Fat 0.8 g, Polyunsaturated Fat 0.8 g,
Cholesterol 0.5 mg, Sodium 127 mg, Fiber 1 g

Creamed Spinach

Mary Ann Lefever, Lancaster, PA
Makes 6 servings

Prep. Time: 15 minutes   ♣   *Cooking/Baking Time: 30–40 minutes*

16-oz. bag frozen chopped baby spinach

Half onion, minced (about ¾ cup)

2 Tbsp. olive oil

¼ tsp. black pepper

½ tsp. garlic powder, or 1 clove garlic, chopped

3 Tbsp. flour

1½ cups skim milk

⅓ cup fat-free half-and-half

¼ cup grated Parmesan cheese

1. Cook spinach in microwave or on stovetop, according to package directions.

2. Drain very well, squeezing out excess water. Set aside.

3. Cook onion in large saucepan or skillet in olive oil until tender.

4. Add pepper, garlic powder, and flour. Cook until beginning to brown.

5. Stir in milk and half-and-half. Cook over low heat, stirring continually, until thickened.

6. Stir in cooked spinach and Parmesan cheese.

7. Coat a 9″ glass pie plate with non-fat cooking spray. Spread spinach mixture in pie plate.

8. Bake uncovered at 300° for 20 minutes.

Per Serving

Calories 120, Kilojoules 502, Protein 6 g,
Carbohydrates 12 g, Total Fat 5 g, Saturated Fat 1.3 g,
Monounsaturated Fat 3.5 g, Polyunsaturated Fat 0.2 g,
Cholesterol 5 mg, Sodium 186 mg, Fiber 2 g

Cucumbers in Yogurt

Charlotte Hagner, Montague, MI
Makes 4 servings

Prep. Time: 20 minutes & *Chilling Time: 1 hour or more*

2 medium cucumbers

1 medium white onion

¼ tsp. salt

⅛ tsp. coarsely ground black pepper

½ cup plain low-fat yogurt

½ tsp. dill weed

4 Romaine lettuce leaves, optional

4 grape or cherry tomatoes, optional

4 radishes, sliced thin, optional

1. Peel cucumbers and make tracks down their sides with tines of a fork. Slice thin.

2. Peel onion and slice very thin into rings.

3. Spread half the cucumber slices in layers over bottom of serving bowl.

4. Follow with half the onion rings.

5. Sprinkle with half the salt, pepper, yogurt, and dill weed. Repeat layers.

6. Refrigerate for at least 1 hour before serving to allow flavors to blend.

7. Bring full bowl to the table, or make 4 individual side salads, each on a leaf of Romaine lettuce garnished with a grape or cherry tomato and/or radish.

Per Serving

Calories 52, Kilojoules 218, Protein 3 g,
Carbohydrates 9 g, Total Fat 1 g, Saturated Fat 0.4 g,
Monounsaturated Fat 0.3 g, Polyunsaturated Fat 0.3 g,
Cholesterol 2 mg, Sodium 171 mg, Fiber 2 g

Quick Stir-Fried Vegetables

Judith Govotsos, Frederick, MD
Makes 5 servings

Prep. Time: 20 minutes ⚜ *Cooking Time: 7–10 minutes*

4 cloves garlic, sliced thin

4 carrots, sliced thin on angle

1 small yellow squash, sliced thin on angle

1 small green zucchini squash, sliced thin on angle

1 large onion, sliced thin

1 Tbsp. olive oil

¼ tsp. salt

⅛ tsp. pepper

1. Prepare all vegetables. Do not mix together.

2. Place olive oil in large non-stick skillet.

3. Add garlic and carrot. Stir-fry 2–3 minutes

4. Add remainder of vegetables. Cook and stir until just lightly cooked, about 5–7 more minutes.

5. Stir in seasonings and serve.

Per Serving

Calories 98, Kilojoules 410, Protein 2 g,
Carbohydrates 16 g, Total Fat 3 g, Saturated Fat 0.4 g,
Monounsaturated Fat 2 g, Polyunsaturated Fat 0.6 g,
Cholesterol 0 mg, Sodium 194 mg, Fiber 4 g

Lemony Garlic Asparagus

SLOW COOKER

Hope Comerford, Clinton Township, MI
Makes 4 servings

Prep. Time: 5 minutes ⚬ *Cooking Time: 1½–2 hours* ⚬ *Ideal slow cooker size: 2- or 3-qt.*

1 lb. asparagus, bottom inch (tough part) removed

1 Tbsp. olive oil

1½ Tbsp. lemon juice

3–4 cloves garlic, peeled and minced

¼ tsp. salt

⅛ tsp. pepper

1. Spray crock with non-stick spray.

2. Lay asparagus at bottom of crock and coat with the olive oil.

3. Pour the lemon juice over the top, then sprinkle with the garlic, salt, and pepper.

4. Cover and cook on low for 1½–2 hours.

Serving suggestion:
Garnish with diced pimento, garlic, and lemon zest.

Per Serving
Calories 58, Kilojoules 241, Protein 3 g,
Carbohydrates 6 g, Total Fat 4 g, Saturated Fat 0.5 g,
Monounsaturated Fat 2 g, Polyunsaturated Fat 0.4 g,
Cholesterol 0 mg, Sodium 123 mg, Fiber 2 g

Scalloped Cheesy Tomatoes

Scarlett Von Bernuth, Canon City, CO
Makes 6 servings

Prep. Time: 15 minutes & Baking Time: 35 minutes

4 fresh tomatoes, sliced, divided

1 cup soft bread cubes, divided

1 Tbsp. fresh parsley, divided

2 Tbsp. olive oil, divided

½ cup cracker crumbs (made from crackers with unsalted tops)

¼ cup low-sodium, low-fat grated cheese

Pepper

1. Fill a lightly greased baking dish with alternate layers of tomatoes and bread cubes.

2. Sprinkle parsley and olive oil over each layer.

3. Cover top with cracker crumbs. Sprinkle with cheese.

4. Bake uncovered in 350°–375° oven for 35 minutes.

Tip:

To easily and cleanly crush crackers, put them in a plastic bag. Then crush them with a rolling pin.

Per Serving

Calories 126, Kilojoules 527, Protein 4 g, Carbohydrates 18 g, Total Fat 4 g, Saturated Fat 1 g, Monounsaturated Fat 2 g, Polyunsaturated Fat 1 g, Cholesterol 3 mg, Sodium 200 mg, Fiber 2 g

Roasted Summer Vegetables

Moreen Weaver, Bath, NY
Makes 6 servings

Prep. Time: 20–30 minutes ⚘ *Baking Time: 20 minutes*

8–10 cups fresh vegetables: your choice of any summer squash, onions, potatoes, tomatoes, green beans, broccoli, cauliflower, carrots, green or red bell sweet peppers, mild chili peppers, eggplant, mushrooms, or fennel

Seasoning 1:

3 Tbsp. fresh basil, chopped

2 Tbsp. fresh cilantro, chopped

1 ½ Tbsp. fresh thyme, chopped

1 Tbsp. olive oil

½ tsp. pepper

3 cloves garlic, minced

Seasoning 2:

4 cloves garlic, minced

1 Tbsp. olive oil

2 Tbsp. fresh thyme

2 Tbsp. fresh oregano

2 Tbsp. fresh basil, chopped

2 Tbsp. balsamic vinegar

1 Tbsp. Dijon mustard

¼ tsp. pepper

1. Cut vegetables into bite-sized pieces for even cooking. For example, slice potatoes thinly, but chop summer squash in chunks. Place prepared vegetables in large mixing bowl as you go.

2. Toss vegetables with one of the seasoning options.

3. Spread seasoned vegetables in a thin layer on a lightly greased baking sheet with sides.

4. Bake in preheated oven at 425° for 20 minutes. Stir occasionally.

Per Serving
Calories 99, Kilojoules 414, Protein 3 g,
Carbohydrates 17 g, Total Fat 2.6 g, Saturated Fat 0.3 g,
Monounsaturated Fat 1.7 g, Polyunsaturated Fat 0.6 g,
Cholesterol 0 mg, Sodium 95 mg, Fiber 4 g

Oven Fries

Sherry H. Kauffman, Minot, ND
Makes 6 servings

Prep. Time: 15 minutes ☙ *Baking Time: 25 minutes*

3 medium unpeeled baking potatoes
(1 ½ lb.)

2 large carrots, peeled

2 tsp. vegetable, or canola, oil

¼ tsp. salt

¼ tsp. pepper

non-fat cooking spray

1. Scrub potatoes. Cut potatoes and carrots into 3½" × ½" strips. Pat dry with paper towel.

2. Combine oil, salt, and pepper in large bowl. Add potatoes and carrots. Toss to coat.

3. Arrange in a single layer on a baking sheet coated with non-fat cooking spray.

4. Bake at 475° for 25 minutes, or until tender and brown, turning after 15 minutes.

Per Serving

Calories 111, Kilojoules 464, Protein 3 g,
Carbohydrates 21 g, Total Fat 2 g, Saturated Fat 0.5 g,
Monounsaturated Fat 1 g, Polyunsaturated Fat 0.5 g,
Cholesterol 0 mg, Sodium 117 mg, Fiber 2 g

Easy Spicy Oven French Fries

Trudy Kutter, Corfu, NY
Makes 8 servings

Prep. Time: 15 minutes ❧ Baking Time: 25–30 minutes

1¼ lb. potatoes, scrubbed, but unpeeled

2 tsp. chili powder

2 tsp. minced garlic

¼ tsp. salt

1. Heat oven to 450°. Spray jelly-roll baking pan with non-stick cooking spray.

2. Cut potatoes into about ½"-thick sticks. Put in mixing bowl.

3. Toss julienned potatoes with chili powder, garlic, and salt.

4. Spread in prepared baking pan.

5. Bake until crisp, browned, and tender, about 25–30 minutes.

Tip:

If your family does not care for garlic or chili powder, try a bit of paprika, or use herbs such as oregano or thyme.

Per Serving

Calories 70, Kilojoules 293, Protein 2 g,
Carbohydrates 15 g, Total Fat trace, Saturated Fat trace,
Monounsaturated Fat trace, Polyunsaturated Fat trace,
Cholesterol 0 mg, Sodium 84 mg, Fiber 2 g

Guilt-Free Golden Mashed Potatoes

Sharon Wantland, Menomonee Falls, WI
Makes 8 servings

Prep. Time: 30 minutes ☙ Cooking/Baking Time: 40–45 minutes

2 lb. Yukon Gold potatoes

2 reduced-sodium chicken bouillon cubes

¼ cup skim milk

Half an 8-oz. pkg. fat-free cream cheese, softened

¼ cup fat-free sour cream

½ cup low-fat shredded sharp cheddar cheese

¼ tsp. white pepper

2 tsp. chopped fresh parsley

1. Peel and cut potatoes into small cubes. Place in 4-quart saucepan with bouillon and water to cover.

2. Cover pan. Bring to a boil and cook until very tender, about 30 minutes.

3. Drain and return potatoes to pan.

4. Preheat oven to 425°.

5. Mash potatoes with electric mixer or hand-held ricer.

6. Add all remaining ingredients to potatoes except parsley. Mix well.

7. Place 6 oval-shaped mounds of potatoes on cookie sheet, lightly covered with vegetable spray coating.

8. Bake in preheated oven 10–15 minutes, or until golden brown.

9. Garnish with parsley just before serving.

Per Serving

Calories 118, Kilojoules 494, Protein 6 g,
Carbohydrates 22 g, Total Fat 0.5 g, Saturated Fat 0.3 g,
Monounsaturated Fat 0.1 g, Polyunsaturated Fat 0.1 g,
Cholesterol 3 mg, Sodium 200 mg, Fiber 2 g

Dutch Potato Salad

Jean Harris Robinson, Cinnaminson, NJ
Makes 8 servings

Prep. Time: 15 minutes & Cooking Time: 15 minutes

2 lb. small red potatoes

3 qts. cold water

4 slices lean bacon

½ cup thinly sliced red onion

2 Tbsp. olive oil

¼ cup apple cider vinegar

Pinch of sugar

Dash of black pepper

½ Tbsp. chopped fresh parsley

1. Cut cleaned potatoes into bite-sized pieces. Place in saucepan and bring to a boil in 3 quarts cold water.

2. Cook about 10 minutes. Drain potatoes, reserving ⅓ cup cooking liquid (important!).

3. Meanwhile, cook bacon until crisp. Drain well on paper towel.

4. Put cooked potatoes into serving bowl. Add sliced onion and stir through.

5. Pour bacon drippings out of pan. Cool pan, and then blot pan with paper towel.

6. Add oil, vinegar, sugar, and reserved potato water to pan. Cook over low heat for one minute, stirring to loosen brown residue left from bacon.

7. Pour dressing over potatoes. Stir and serve warm.

8. Add crumbled bacon just before serving.

Per Serving

Calories 156, Kilojoules 653, Protein 4 g,
Carbohydrates 23 g, Total Fat 5 g, Saturated Fat 1 g,
Monounsaturated Fat 3 g, Polyunsaturated Fat 1 g,
Cholesterol 4 mg, Sodium 105 mg, Fiber 2 g

Sweet Potato Casserole

Joyce Shackelford, Green Bay, WI
Makes 6 servings

Prep. Time: 20 minutes ❧ *Cooking/Baking Time: 1 hour*

4 medium sweet potatoes

1 Tbsp. olive oil

¼ cup freshly squeezed orange juice

2 Tbsp. chopped walnuts, plus 2 tsp. for garnish

¼ tsp. nutmeg

1. Cook whole sweet potatoes in boiling water in a covered saucepan 25–30 minutes, or until tender. Drain.

2. Allow potatoes to cool enough to hold. Then peel and mash in a mixer or with a hand-held ricer.

3. Add olive oil, orange juice, 2 Tbsp. chopped walnuts, and nutmeg. Mix thoroughly.

4. Place in lightly greased 1-quart baking dish. Garnish with 2 tsp. chopped walnuts.

5. Bake uncovered at 375° for 25 minutes.

Per Serving

Calories 120, Kilojoules 502, Protein 2 g, Carbohydrates 18 g, Total Fat 4 g, Saturated Fat 0.5 g, Monounsaturated Fat 2 g, Polyunsaturated Fat 1.5 g, Cholesterol 0 mg, Sodium 48 mg, Fiber 3 g

Thyme Roasted Sweet Potatoes

SLOW COOKER

Hope Comerford, Clinton Township, MI
Makes 6 servings

Prep. Time: 20 minutes ⚭ *Cooking Time: 7 hours* ⚭ *Ideal slow cooker size: 4-qt.*

4–6 medium sweet potatoes, peeled, cubed

3 Tbsp. olive oil

5–6 large garlic cloves, minced

⅓ cup fresh thyme leaves

½ tsp. kosher salt

¼ tsp. red pepper flakes

1. Place all ingredients into the crock and stir.

2. Cover and cook on low for 7 hours, or until potatoes are tender.

Per Serving

Calories 178, Kilojoules 745, Protein 2 g,
Carbohydrates 28 g, Total Fat 7 g, Saturated Fat 1 g,
Monounsaturated Fat 5 g, Polyunsaturated Fat 1 g,
Cholesterol 0 mg, Sodium 232 mg, Fiber 4 g

Healthy Sweet Potato Fries

Gladys M. High, Ephrata, PA
Makes 4 servings

Prep. Time: 15 minutes & Baking Time: 30 minutes

Olive oil cooking spray

2 large sweet potatoes, peeled and cut into wedges

¼ tsp. salt

¼ tsp. black pepper

Freshly chopped oregano, thyme, rosemary, and garlic, optional

1. Preheat oven to 400°.

2. Coat baking sheet with organic olive oil cooking spray.

3. Arrange potato wedges on baking sheet in a single layer. Coat with cooking spray.

4. Sprinkle potatoes with salt, pepper, and any additional optional seasoning of your choice.

5. Roast 30 minutes, or until tender and golden brown.

Per Serving

Calories 56, Kilojoules 234, Protein 1 g, Carbohydrates 13 g, Total Fat trace, Saturated Fat trace, Monounsaturated Fat trace, Polyunsaturated Fat trace, Cholesterol 0 mg, Sodium 181 mg, Fiber 2 g

"Baked" Sweet Potatoes

SLOW COOKER

Hope Comerford, Clinton Township, MI
Makes 5 potatoes

Prep. Time: 2 minutes ⚷ *Cooking Time: 4–5 hours* ⚷ *Ideal slow cooker size: 5- or 6-qt.*

5 sweet potatoes, pierced in several places with a fork or knife

1. Place sweet potatoes in slow cooker.

2. Cover and cook on low for 4–5 hours, or until they are tender when poked with a fork or knife.

Per Serving

Calories 112, Kilojoules 467, Protein 2 g, Carbohydrates 26 g, Total Fat 0 g, Saturated Fat 0 g, Monounsaturated Fat 0 g, Polyunsaturated Fat 0 g, Cholesterol 0 mg, Sodium 72 mg, Fiber 4g

Squash Apple Bake

Lavina Hochstedler, Grand Blanc, MI
Makes 6 main-dish servings

Prep. Time: 30 minutes & *Baking Time: 45–50 minutes*

4 cups cubed butternut squash, divided

3 Tbsp. honey, or brown sugar

⅓ cup orange, or apple, juice

2 tsp. cornstarch

2–3 apples, cut in short thick slices, divided

¼ cup raisins, divided

Cinnamon

1 Tbsp. soft-tub margarine, non-hydrogenated

1. Slice butternut squash into ¾" rounds. Peel and cut into cubes.

2. Combine honey, juice, and cornstarch in a small bowl.

3. In greased 2- or 3-quart baking dish, layer in half the squash, followed by a layer of half the apples, and then a layer of half the raisins.

4. Repeat layers.

5. Sprinkle generously with cinnamon.

6. Pour juice mixture over all.

7. Dot with margarine.

8. Cover and bake at 350° for 45–50 minutes, or until tender. Serve warm as a vegetable.

Per Serving

Calories 150, Kilojoules 628, Protein 1 g,
Carbohydrates 33 g, Total Fat 2 g, Saturated Fat 0.2 g,
Monounsaturated Fat 0.8 g, Polyunsaturated Fat 1 g,
Cholesterol 0 mg, Sodium 31 mg, Fiber 4 g

Spicy Roasted Butternut Squash

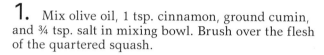

Marilyn Mowry, Irving, TX
Makes 15–20 servings

Prep. Time: 1 hour & Cooking Time: 4–6 hours & Ideal slow cooker size: 6-qt.

¼ cup olive oil

2 tsp. ground cinnamon, divided

½ tsp. ground cumin

1¾ tsp. salt, divided

5-lb. butternut squash, split in quarters and seeds removed

2 carrots, diced

1 large white onion, diced

2 Granny Smith apples, peeled, cored, and quartered

4 chipotles in adobo sauce, seeds scraped out, chopped roughly

10 cups gluten-free chicken stock

1. Mix olive oil, 1 tsp. cinnamon, ground cumin, and ¾ tsp. salt in mixing bowl. Brush over the flesh of the quartered squash.

2. Place squash cut side down on a rimmed baking sheet lined with foil.

3. Add carrots, onion, and apples to bowl with oil and toss. Spread on another foil-lined sheet.

4. Roast both trays 40–50 minutes at 425° until squash is soft and onion mix is golden brown. Scoop out the squash.

5. Put squash, veggie mix, chipotles, 1 tsp. salt, and 1 tsp. cinnamon in slow cooker. Add chicken broth.

6. Cover and cook on high 4 hours or low for 6 hours. Mash with a potato masher or puree with immersion blender.

Per Serving

Calories 109, Kilojoules 457, Protein 4 g,

Carbohydrates 17 g, Total Fat 4 g, Saturated Fat 1 g,

Monounsaturated Fat 2 g, Polyunsaturated Fat 0.3 g,

Cholesterol 0 mg, Sodium 396 mg, Fiber 3 g

Beverages and Desserts

Blueberry-Pomegranate Smoothie

Dena Tompkins, Huntersville, NC
Makes 2 servings

Prep. Time: 10 minutes

1 cup skim milk

1 cup fresh or frozen blueberries

Seeds from 1 small-medium pomegranate

1 Tbsp. lemon juice

1 Tbsp. honey

6–8 ice cubes (if using frozen berries omit ice cubes)

1. Combine all ingredients except ice cubes in blender. Blend well.

2. Gradually add ice cubes (unless using frozen berries). Continue blending until smooth enough to draw up with straw.

Per Serving

Calories 169, Kilojoules 707, Protein 5 g,
Carbohydrates 38 g, Total Fat 0.4 g, Saturated Fat 0.2 g,
Monounsaturated Fat 0.1 g, Polyunsaturated Fat 0.1 g,
Cholesterol 2.4 mg, Sodium 58 mg, Fiber 2 g

Four Fruit Yogurt Smoothie

Janet Oberholtzer, Ephrata, PA
Makes 4 servings

Prep. Time: 10 minutes

1 cup frozen unsweetened strawberries

1 cup frozen unsweetened peaches

¾ cup frozen unsweetened blueberries

1 large ripe banana

1 cup fat-free peach, or strawberry, yogurt, sweetened with low-calorie sweetener

1 cup skim milk

1. Combine all ingredients in blender or food processor.

2. Process until smooth, stopping to scrape sides and push ingredients down into blender as needed.

3. Pour into serving glasses.

Per Serving

Calories 119, Kilojoules 498, Protein 5 g, Carbohydrates 24 g, Total Fat 0.5 g, Saturated Fat 0.2 g, Monounsaturated Fat 0.1 g, Polyunsaturated Fat 0.2 g, Cholesterol 2 mg, Sodium 60 mg, Fiber 3 g

Peaches and Cream Power Shake

Virginia Graybill, Hershey, PA
Makes 2 servings

Prep. Time: 20 minutes ♣ Chilling Time: 1 hour

¼ cup boiling water

1 peach-flavored tea bag

1¼ cups diced fresh peaches

¾ cup low-fat plain yogurt

2 Tbsp. honey

1 Tbsp. soy protein powder, optional,
not included in analyses

½ Tbsp. ground flaxseed

1 cup ice cubes

1. Pour boiling water over tea bag in teapot or small saucepan to make tea concentrate.

2. Let stand a few minutes to steep. Remove bag.

3. Chill liquid for an hour in the fridge.

4. Combine chilled tea concentrate with remaining ingredients in blender.

5. Whirl until smooth.

Tip:

Make several batches of tea concentrate ahead of time and keep on hand in the refrigerator.

Per Serving
Calories 162, Kilojoules 678, Protein 6 g,
Carbohydrates 33 g, Total Fat 1 g, Saturated Fat 0.1 g,
Monounsaturated Fat 0.3 g, Polyunsaturated Fat 0.6 g,
Cholesterol 2 mg, Sodium 74 mg, Fiber 2 g

V-5 Juice

Anita King, Bellefontaine, OH
Makes 8 servings

Prep. Time: 30 minutes ⚜ *Cooking Time: 45 minutes* ⚜ *Cooling Time: 3 hours*

5 lb. ripe tomatoes, chopped

½ cup water

¼ cup chopped green bell sweet pepper

¼ cup chopped carrot

¼ cup chopped celery

¼ cup lemon juice

2 Tbsp. chopped onion

½ tsp. salt

1–1½ small serrano pepper, optional, not included in analyses

1. Combine all ingredients in large soup pot.

2. Bring to a boil. Reduce heat, cover, and simmer 30 minutes.

3. Allow to cool to room temperature.

4. Press through food mill or Victorio strainer.

5. Refrigerate until chilled.

6. Shake or stir before serving.

Per Serving

Calories 57, Kilojoules 238, Protein 3 g,
Carbohydrates 11 g, Total Fat 0.5 g, Saturated Fat 0.1 g,
Monounsaturated Fat 0.15 g, Polyunsaturated Fat 0.25 g,
Cholesterol 0 mg, Sodium 165 mg, Fiber 4 g

Frozen Dream Pops

Janelle Reitz, Lancaster, PA

Makes 8 servings; 1 pop/serving

Prep. Time: 10 minutes ❧ Freezing Time: 6 hours

6-oz. can unsweetened orange juice
concentrate, thawed slightly

2 cups low-fat plain yogurt

1 tsp. vanilla extract

1. Mix fruit juice concentrate and yogurt together in a bowl.

2. Pour into 8 popsicle molds. (You can also use 3-oz. paper cups. Cover each with foil. Insert plastic spoons or wooden sticks through the foil.)

3. Freeze until solid.

Per Serving

Calories 74, Kilojoules 310, Protein 4 g,
Carbohydrates 12 g, Total Fat 1 g, Saturated Fat 0.6 g,
Monounsaturated Fat 0.2 g, Polyunsaturated Fat 0.2 g,
Cholesterol 4 mg, Sodium 43 mg, Fiber trace

Banana Orange Pops

Kathy Keener Shantz, Lancaster, PA
Makes 12 servings; 1 pop/serving

Prep. Time: 10 minutes   ⚭   Freezing Time: 3–4 hours

2 ripe bananas

6 oz. (¾ cup) orange juice concentrate, slightly thawed

12 oz. silken soft tofu

1. Combine all ingredients in food processor or blender. Blend until smooth.

2. Pour into 12 popsicle molds, or 12 3-oz. paper cups.

3. Place in freezer. If using paper cups, remove after 1 hour and insert a wooden stick in center of each cup. Return to freezer.

4. Freeze until solid.

Tip:

Peel ripe bananas and freeze for later use.

Per Serving
Calories 55, Kilojoules 230. Protein 2 g,
Carbohydrates 10 g, Total Fat trace, Saturated Fat trace,
Monounsaturated Fat trace, Polyunsaturated Fat trace,
Cholesterol 0 mg, Sodium 2 mg, Fiber 0.5 g

Red, White, and Blue Parfait

Becky Gehman, Bergton, VA
Makes 4 servings

Prep. Time: 15 minutes

Creamy Filling:

1 cup low-fat vanilla yogurt, sweetened
with low-calorie sweetener

¼ cup fat-free cream cheese
(Neufchatel), softened

1 tsp. honey

Fruit:

1 pint fresh strawberries, sliced, divided

1½ cups fresh blueberries, divided

1. Make creamy filling by placing yogurt, cream cheese, and honey into bowl. Beat until fluffy.

2. Assemble parfaits by placing ⅓ cup strawberries in each of 6 parfait glasses.

3. Top each with 3 Tbsp. creamy filling.

4. Top that with ¼ cup blueberries in each glass.

5. Garnish each by dividing remaining topping.

6. Chill until ready to serve.

Per Serving

Calories 100, Kilojoules 418, Protein 5 g,
Carbohydrates 20 g, Total Fat 1 g, Saturated Fat 0.4 g,
Monounsaturated Fat 0.2 g, Polyunsaturated Fat 0.4 g,
Cholesterol 2 mg, Sodium 116 mg, Fiber 3 g

Strawberry Fluff

Shari Ladd, Hudson, MI
Makes 6 servings

Prep. Time: 15 minutes   ⚬   Chilling Time: 2–3 hours

.3-oz. pkg. sugar-free strawberry gelatin

Creamy Filling:

1 cup low-fat vanilla yogurt, sweetened with low-calorie sweetener

¼ cup fat-free cream cheese (Neufchatel), softened

1 tsp. honey

¼ whole angel food cake, cut into cubes

3 cups sliced fresh strawberries

1. Prepare gelatin according to package directions. Refrigerate 1 hour in a good-sized bowl.

2. Meanwhile, make creamy filling by placing yogurt, cream cheese, and honey into bowl. Beat until fluffy.

3. To assemble fluff, scatter pieces of cake evenly in 8″ pan.

4. Layer berries evenly over cake.

5. After gelatin has been refrigerated for 1 hour, whip creamy filling into gelatin.

6. Spoon over berries.

7. Cover and chill until set, about another hour or so.

Per Serving

Calories 136, Kilojoules 569, Protein 5 g,
Carbohydrates 19 g, Total Fat 4.5 g, Saturated Fat 3 g,
Monounsaturated Fat 1 g, Polyunsaturated Fat 0.5 g,
Cholesterol 14 mg, Sodium 200 mg, Fiber 2 g

Coconut Rice Pudding

SLOW COOKER

Hope Comerford, Clinton Township, MI
Makes 6 servings

Prep. Time: 5 minutes ⚬ *Cooking Time: 2½ hours* ⚬ *Ideal slow cooker size: 5- or 6-qt.*

2½ cups low-fat milk
14-oz. can light coconut milk
½ cup turbinado sugar
1 cup Arborio rice
1 stick cinnamon
1 cup dried cranberries, optional

1. Spray crock with non-stick spray.

2. In crock, whisk together the milk, coconut milk, and sugar.

3. Add in the rice and cinnamon stick.

4. Cover and cook on low about 2–2½ hours, or until rice is tender and the pudding has thickened.

5. Remove cinnamon stick. If using cranberries, sprinkle on top of each bowl of Coconut Rice Pudding.

Per Serving
Calories 355, Kilojoules 1486, Protein 7 g, Carbohydrates 73 g, Total Fat 5 g, Saturated Fat 4 g, Monounsaturated Fat 0 g, Polyunsaturated Fat 0 g, Cholesterol 5 mg, Sodium 60 mg, Fiber 3 g

Orange Panna Cotta

Marilyn Mowry, Irving, TX
Makes 4 servings

Prep. Time: 10 minutes ⚜ Cooking Time: 10 minutes ⚜ Chilling Time: 8 hours, or overnight

2 cups evaporated skim milk

1 envelope unflavored gelatin

¼ cup sugar

1 tsp. vanilla extract

1 tsp. orange extract

1 tsp. grated orange peel

Pinch of salt

½ cup fat-free vanilla yogurt, sweetened with low-calorie sweetener

Ground cinnamon

1. Combine milk and gelatin in non-stick pan. Let stand until gelatin softens, about 5 minutes.

2. Cook over low heat, stirring constantly, until gelatin dissolves completely, about 5 minutes.

3. Whisk in sugar, both extracts, orange peel, and salt. Bring to a simmer, stirring frequently.

4. Divide evenly among 4 small ramekins or custard cups.

5. Cool slightly. Then cover and refrigerate overnight.

6. To serve, top each with 2 Tbsp. fat-free vanilla yogurt and a sprinkle of cinnamon.

Per Serving
Calories 185, Kilojoules 774, Protein 12 g,
Carbohydrates 31 g, Total Fat 1 g, Saturated Fat 0.2 g,
Monounsaturated Fat 0.7 g, Polyunsaturated Fat 0.1 g,
Cholesterol 7 mg, Sodium 168 mg, Fiber trace

Banana Mousse

Lois Hess, Lancaster, PA
Makes 4 servings

Prep. Time: 15 minutes ♣ Chilling Time: 2 hours

3 Tbsp. skim milk
1 medium banana, cut in quarters
4 tsp. sugar
1 tsp. vanilla extract
1 cup plain low-fat yogurt
1 banana cut into 8 slices

1. Place milk, medium banana cut in quarters, sugar, and vanilla into blender. Process for 15 seconds at high speed until smooth.

2. Pour mixture into small bowl. Fold in yogurt.

3. Chill two hours.

4. Spoon into four dessert dishes.

5. Garnish each dish of mousse with two banana slices just before serving.

Per Serving
Calories 108, Kilojoules 452, Protein 4 g,
Carbohydrates 21 g, Total Fat 1 g, Saturated Fat 0.25 g,
Monounsaturated Fat 0.5 g, Polyunsaturated Fat 0.25 g,
Cholesterol 3 mg, Sodium 48 mg, Fiber 1.5 g

Mocha Chiffon Pie

Ann Bender, New Hope, VA
Makes 8 servings

Prep. Time: 15 minutes & *Cooking Time: 5 minutes* & *Cooling Time: 2–3 hours*

1 Tbsp. plain gelatin

¼ cup cold water

½ cup sugar

2 Tbsp. cocoa powder, unsweetened

1 tsp. dry instant coffee

⅛ tsp. salt

1½ cups evaporated skim milk

8 Tbsp. light frozen whipped topping, thawed

1. In a small bowl, dissolve gelatin in cold water.

2. Mix sugar, cocoa powder, dry coffee, and salt in saucepan.

3. Stir milk into saucepan. Heat to boiling, stirring frequently.

4. Add gelatin mixture and stir until dissolved.

5. Cool in fridge until mixture is slightly congealed.

6. Pour into 9″ pie pan.

7. Cool in fridge until completely set.

8. Serve each pie wedge topped with 1 Tbsp. whipped topping.

Per Serving

Calories 111, Kilojoules 464, Protein 7 g,
Carbohydrates 19 g, Total Fat 1 g, Saturated Fat 0.5 g,
Monounsaturated Fat 0.3 g, Polyunsaturated Fat 0.2 g,
Cholesterol 2 mg, Sodium 100 mg, Fiber trace

Cheesecake

Sharon Shank, Bridgewater, VA
Makes 8 servings

Prep. Time: 15 minutes ⚶ *Cooling Time: 2–3 hours*

2 Tbsp. cold water

I envelope unflavored gelatin

2 Tbsp. lemon juice

½ cup skim milk, heated almost to boiling

Egg substitute equivalent to I egg, or 2 egg whites

¼ cup sugar

I tsp. vanilla extract

2 cups low-fat cottage cheese

Lemon zest, optional

1. Combine water, gelatin, and lemon juice in blender container. Process on low speed 1–2 minutes to soften gelatin.

2. Add hot milk, processing until gelatin is dissolved.

3. Add egg substitute, sugar, vanilla, and cheese to blender container. Process on high speed until smooth.

4. Pour into 9" pie plate or round flat dish.

5. Refrigerate 2–3 hours.

6. If you wish, top with grated lemon zest just before serving.

Per Serving

Calories 80, Kilojoules 335, Protein 9 g, Carbohydrates 10 g. Total Fat trace, Saturated Fat trace, Monounsaturated Fat trace, Polyunsaturated Fat trace, Cholesterol 3 mg, Sodium 200 mg, Fiber trace

Chocolate Chip Meringue Drops

Bonnie Whaling, Clearfield, PA
Makes 40 cookies, 3 cookies/serving

Prep. Time: 15–20 minutes ❧ Baking Time: 1 hour ❧ Standing Time: 2 hours

2 large egg whites
½ cup sugar
1 tsp vanilla extract
3 Tbsp. cocoa powder, unsweetened
½ cup semi-sweet mini chocolate chips

1. Preheat oven to 250°.

2. Line 2 baking sheets with parchment paper or aluminum foil. Set aside.

3. In large mixer bowl, beat egg whites until they hold stiff peaks.

4. Beat in sugar one tablespoon at a time.

5. Then beat in vanilla.

6. Reduce speed to low and beat in cocoa powder.

7. With a spatula, fold in chocolate chips.

8. Drop batter by rounded teaspoonfuls onto baking sheets, spacing cookies 1" apart.

9. Bake 1 hour.

10. Turn off oven and let cookies remain in oven 2 hours longer.

11. Remove from baking sheets and store in airtight container.

Tip:

Don't make these on a humid day. The mixture will be sticky and hard to handle.

Per Serving

Calories 66, Kilojoules 276, Protein 1 g, Carbohydrates 12 g, Total Fat 2 g, Saturated Fat 0.5 g, Monounsaturated Fat 1 g, Polyunsaturated Fat 0.5 g, Cholesterol 0 mg, Sodium 9 mg, Fiber trace

Fruit-Filled Chocolate Meringues

Gwendolyn Chapman, Gwinn, MI
Makes 6 servings

Prep. Time: 15–20 minutes ❧ Baking Time: 45 minutes ❧ Cooling Time: 1 hour

2 egg whites at room temperature
¼ tsp. cream of tartar
½ tsp. vanilla extract
½ cup sugar
2 Tbsp. dry cocoa powder, unsweetened
3 cups assorted berries and fruit
2 tsp. powdered sugar

1. Preheat oven to 275°.

2. Line cookie sheet with parchment paper.

3. In mixer bowl, beat egg whites with cream of tartar and vanilla until soft peaks form.

4. Beat in sugar one tablespoon at a time until stiff peaks form.

5. Sprinkle cocoa powder over top and fold in gently by hand.

6. Drop by ¼-cup portions onto parchment paper, spacing cookies 1″ apart. Indent each with back of spoon.

7. Bake 45 minutes, or until dry to touch.

8. Remove meringues from oven and cool.

9. Fill center of each cooled meringue with fruit. Sprinkle with powdered sugar. Serve immediately.

Tip:
If fresh berries aren't available, use thawed frozen raspberries.

Per Serving

Calories 110, Kilojoules 460, Protein 2 g,
Carbohydrates 25 g, Total Fat 0.4 g, Saturated Fat 0.1 g,
Monounsaturated Fat 0.1 g, Polyunsaturated Fat 0.2 g,
Cholesterol trace, Sodium 22 mg, Fiber 4 g

Honey-Milk Balls

Kathy Hertzler, Lancaster, PA
Makes 12 servings; 2 balls/serving

Prep. Time: 15 minutes ⚭ *Chilling Time: 15 minutes*

½ cup honey

1 cup natural peanut butter (if you wish, make your own by grinding peanuts)

2 cups instant non-fat dry milk powder

1. Mix honey and peanut butter in medium bowl. Stir until well mixed.

2. Add dry milk, stirring until well combined. You may need to use your fingers.

3. Chill about 15 minutes in fridge.

4. Roll into balls the size of small walnuts.

5. Place in airtight container and keep chilled in refrigerator until ready to serve.

Per Serving

Calories 153, Kilojoules 640, Protein 7 g,
Carbohydrates 19 g, Total Fat 5 g, Saturated Fat 1 g,
Monounsaturated Fat 3 g, Polyunsaturated Fat 1 g,
Cholesterol 2 mg, Sodium 103 mg, Fiber 0.6 g

Apple Walnut Cookies

Rhonda Burgoon, Collingswood, NJ
Makes 36 cookies; 2 cookies/serving

Prep. Time: 20 minutes   Baking Time: 10–12 minutes

1 cup dry rolled oats
½ cup walnuts, chopped
1 cup whole wheat pastry flour
½ tsp. baking soda
¼ tsp. baking powder
¼ tsp. salt
½ tsp. ground cinnamon
¼ tsp. ground ginger
2 egg whites
1 Granny Smith apple peeled, cored, and grated
¼ cup unsweetened applesauce
½ cup light brown sugar, packed
2 Tbsp. canola oil
½ tsp. vanilla extract
½ cup raisins

Tip:
Store in an airtight container for up to 2 days.

1. Heat oven to 375°. Spray 2 baking sheets with non-stick cooking spray.

2. Place oats and nuts on separate unsprayed baking sheets. Toast in oven until golden, about 8 minutes. Set aside.

3. Meanwhile, combine flour, baking soda, baking powder, salt, cinnamon, and ginger in a medium bowl.

4. In a large bowl, combine egg whites, grated apple, applesauce, brown sugar, oil, and vanilla.

5. Stir in combined dry ingredients until well blended.

6. Stir in raisins, oats, and nuts.

7. Drop dough onto prepared baking sheets by tablespoonfuls placed 2" apart.

8. Bake 10–12 minutes, or until cookies are lightly browned.

9. Cool on wire racks for 3 minutes. Cool completely before serving.

Per Serving

Calories 119, Kilojoules 498, Protein 3 g,
Carbohydrates 18 g, Total Fat 4 g, Saturated Fat 0.3 g,
Monounsaturated Fat 1.7 g, Polyunsaturated Fat 2 g,
Cholesterol 0 mg, Sodium 81 mg, Fiber 2 g

Baked Apples with Dates

SLOW COOKER

Mary E. Wheatley, Mashpee, MA
Makes 8 servings

Prep. Time: 20–25 minutes ⚗ Cooking Time: 2–6 hours
Ideal slow cooker size: 6-qt. oval, or large enough cooker that the apples
can each sit on the floor of the cooker, rather than being stacked

8 medium-sized baking apples
Filling:
¾ cup coarsely chopped dates
3 Tbsp. chopped pecans
¼ cup honey
Topping:
1 tsp. ground cinnamon
½ tsp. ground nutmeg
1 Tbsp. coconut oil, melted
½ cup water

1. Wash, core, and peel top third of apples.

2. Mix dates and chopped nuts with honey. Stuff into centers of apples where cores had been.

3. Set apples upright in slow cooker.

4. Sprinkle with cinnamon and nutmeg. Pour melted coconut oil evenly over each apple.

5. Add water around inside edge of cooker.

6. Cover. Cook on low 4–6 hours or on high 2–3 hours, or until apples are as tender as you like them.

Per Serving
Calories 233, Kilojoules 977, Protein 2 g,
Carbohydrates 46 g, Total Fat 6 g, Saturated Fat 2 g,
Monounsaturated Fat 2 g, Polyunsaturated Fat 1 g,
Cholesterol 0 mg, Sodium 3 mg, Fiber 7 g

Apple Dessert

Elaine Good, Lititz, PA
Makes 10 servings

Prep. Time: 20 minutes   ☙   Baking Time: 45 minutes

¼ cup trans-fat-free buttery spread

¾ cup brown sugar

¾ cup whole wheat pastry flour

I tsp. cinnamon

2 Tbsp. shredded coconut, optional, not included in analyses

2 Tbsp. chopped nuts, optional, not included in analyses

8 cups sliced apples

1. Heat oven to 350°.

2. Place buttery spread in 10" pie plate. Place in oven to melt.

3. In a separate bowl, combine sugar, flour, and cinnamon, and coconut and nuts if you wish.

4. Stir dry ingredients into melted spread until crumbs form.

5. Remove about half of crumbs. Set aside.

6. Spread remaining crumbs evenly over bottom of pie plate.

7. Add apple slices to pie plate, mounding up as needed to fill pan.

8. Carefully top with reserved crumbs.

9. Bake 45 minutes. Serve warm with milk if you wish (not included in analyses).

Per Serving

Calories 114, Kilojoules 477, Protein 1 g,
Carbohydrates 17 g, Total Fat 5 g, Saturated Fat 1 g,
Monounsaturated Fat 1 g, Polyunsaturated Fat 3 g,
Cholesterol 0 mg, Sodium 62 mg, Fiber 3 g

Low-Fat Rhubarb Bars

Kathy Rodkey, Halifax, PA
Makes 20 bars; 1 bar/serving

Prep. Time: 20 minutes ❧ *Baking Time: 45 minutes*

1 cup flour
½ cup dry All-Bran cereal
1 cup uncooked rolled oats
1 tsp. baking soda
¼ tsp. salt
¾ cup lightly packed brown sugar
2 egg whites
½ cup low-fat sour cream
1 tsp. vanilla extract
2 cups cut-up rhubarb

Topping:
⅓ cup lightly packed brown sugar
½ cup chopped nuts
1 tsp. cinnamon
2 Tbsp. canola oil

1. Mix all ingredients together in order as listed, except topping ingredients, in a good-sized bowl.

2. Spread into 9 x 13 baking pan, generously greased with non-stick cooking spray.

3. Mix topping ingredients in a small bowl.

4. Sprinkle over bars.

5. Bake at 350° for 45 minutes.

Per Serving
Calories 108, Kilojoules 452, Protein 3 g,
Carbohydrates 16 g, Total Fat 3.5 g, Saturated Fat 0.2 g,
Monounsaturated Fat 1.5 g, Polyunsaturated Fat 1.8 g,
Cholesterol trace, Sodium 113 mg, Fiber 2 g

Healthy Coconut Apple Crisp

SLOW COOKER

Hope Comerford, Clinton Township, MI
Makes 8–9 servings

Prep. Time: 20 minutes ⚬ *Cooking Time: 2 hours* ⚬ *Ideal slow cooker size: 3- or 4-qt.*

5 medium Granny Smith apples, peeled, cored, sliced

1 Tbsp. cinnamon

¼ tsp. nutmeg

1 tsp. vanilla extract

Crumble:

1 cup gluten-free oats

½ cup coconut flour

½ cup unsweetened coconut flakes

1 tsp. cinnamon

⅛ tsp. nutmeg

½ tsp. sea salt

2 Tbsp. honey

2 Tbsp. coconut oil, melted

2–3 Tbsp. unsweetened coconut milk

1. Spray crock with non-stick spray

2. In the crock, combine apple slices, cinnamon, nutmeg, and vanilla.

3. In a medium bowl, combine all of the crumble ingredients. If too dry, add a bit more honey or coconut milk. Pour over top of apple mixture.

4. Cover slow cooker and cook on low for 2 hours.

Serving suggestion:

Serve with a scoop of coconut ice cream.

Per Serving

Calories 157, Kilojoules 657, Protein 3 g,
Carbohydrates 18 g, Total Fat 6 g, Saturated Fat 5 g,
Monounsaturated Fat 0 g, Polyunsaturated Fat 0 g,
Cholesterol 0 mg, Sodium 117 mg, Fiber 4 g

Quick Yummy Peaches

SLOW COOKER

Willard E. Roth, Elkhart, IN
Makes 6 servings

Prep. Time: 5–20 minutes ♣ Cooking Time: 5 hours ♣ Ideal slow cooker size: 3-qt.

⅓ cup low-fat gluten-free baking mix
⅔ cup gluten-free oats
⅓ cup maple syrup
1 tsp ground cinnamon
4 cups sliced fresh peaches
½ cup water

1. Mix together baking mix, oats, maple syrup, and cinnamon in greased slow cooker.

2. Stir in peaches and water.

3. Cook on low for at least 5 hours. (If you like a drier cobbler, remove lid for last 15–30 minutes of cooking.)

Per Serving

Calories 169, Kilojoules 705, Protein 4 g,
Carbohydrates 38 g, Total Fat 1 g, Saturated Fat 0 g,
Monounsaturated Fat 0 g, Polyunsaturated Fat 0 g,
Cholesterol 0 mg, Sodium 347 mg, Fiber 4 g

Peach-Rhubarb Crisp

Dorothy VanDeest, Memphis, TN
Makes 6 servings

Prep. Time: 15 minutes ⚬ *Baking Time: 35–40 minutes*

5 cups peeled, sliced fresh peaches, or frozen unsweetened peach slices

1 cup fresh, or frozen, sliced rhubarb

⅓ cup sugar

2 tsp. lemon juice

¼ tsp. apple pie spice, or ground cinnamon

½ cup uncooked rolled oats

⅓ cup packed brown sugar

¼ cup whole wheat pastry flour

¼ tsp. ground cinnamon

¼ cup trans-fat-free buttery spread

2 Tbsp. broken walnuts, or pecans

1. For filling, thaw fruit, if frozen. Do not drain.

2. In large bowl, combine fruit, ⅓ cup sugar, lemon juice, and apple pie spice. Transfer to a 2-quart square baking dish, generously greased with non-stick baking spray.

3. To make topping, combine oats, brown sugar, flour, and cinnamon in a medium bowl.

4. With pastry blender, cut in buttery spread until mixture resembles coarse crumbs.

5. Stir in nuts.

6. Sprinkle over filling in baking dish.

7. Bake at 375° for 35–40 minutes, or until fruit is tender, filling is bubbling around edges, and topping is golden.

Per Serving

Calories 266, Kilojoules 1113, Protein 3 g, Carbohydrates 40 g, Total Fat 10 g, Saturated Fat 2 g, Monounsaturated Fat 3 g, Polyunsaturated Fat 5 g, Cholesterol 0 mg, Sodium 106 mg, Fiber 4 g

Multi-Fruit Crisp

Heidi Roggie, Big Lake, AK
Makes 8 servings

Prep. Time: 20–30 minutes ⚜ *Baking Time: 30 minutes*

1½ cups of 4 fruits, fresh or frozen (a total of 6 cups) — blackberries, raspberries, blueberries, apples, peaches, rhubarb, or others

1¼ cups water

¼ cup sugar

2 Tbsp. cornstarch

¼ cup whole wheat pastry flour

½ cup dry rolled oats

3 Tbsp. canola oil

⅓ cup brown sugar

⅓ cup chopped walnuts, optional, not included in analyses

1. Mix fruit together gently in a large bowl.

2. Spoon into 9 × 13 baking pan, generously greased with non-stick cooking spray.

3. In a saucepan cook water, sugar, and cornstarch together over medium heat, stirring constantly until thickened.

4. Pour mixture over fruit.

5. In the fruit mixing bowl, combine flour, oats, oil, and brown sugar, and nuts if you wish, until crumbly.

6. Sprinkle evenly over fruit.

7. Bake, uncovered, at 375° for 30 minutes, or until fruit bubbles and is soft.

Per Serving

Calories 174, Kilojoules 728, Protein 2 g, Carbohydrates 30 g, Total Fat 5 g, Saturated Fat 0.5 g, Monounsaturated Fat 2.5 g, Polyunsaturated Fat 2 g, Cholesterol 0 mg, Sodium 4 mg, Fiber 3 g

Zucchini Chocolate Chip Bars

SLOW COOKER

Hope Comerford, Clinton Township, MI
Makes 8–10 servings

Prep. Time: 10 minutes   ♣   Cooking Time: 2–3 hours   ♣   Cooling Time: 30 minutes   ♣   Ideal slow cooker size: 5-qt.

3 eggs

¾ cup turbinado sugar

1 cup all-natural applesauce

3 tsp. vanilla extract

3 cups whole wheat flour

1 tsp. baking soda

½ tsp. baking powder

2 tsp. cinnamon

¼ tsp. salt

2 cups peeled and grated zucchini

1 cup dark chocolate chips

½ cup raisins, optional

1. Spray the crock with non-stick spray.

2. Mix together the eggs, sugar, applesauce, and vanilla.

3. In a separate bowl, mix together the flour, baking soda, baking powder, cinnamon, and salt. Add this to the wet mixture and stir just until everything is mixed well.

4. Stir in the zucchini and chocolate chips.

5. Pour this mixture into the crock.

6. Cover and cook on low for 2–3 hours. Let it cool in crock for about 30 minutes, then flip it over onto a serving platter or plate. It should come right out.

Per Serving (without optional raisins)

Calories 295, Kilojoules 1234, Protein 8 g,
Carbohydrates 54 g, Total Fat 6 g, Saturated Fat 3 g,
Monounsaturated Fat 2 g, Polyunsaturated Fat 0 g,
Cholesterol 57 mg, Sodium 200 mg, Fiber 5 g

Fudgy Secret Brownies

SLOW COOKER

Juanita Weaver, Johnsonville, IL
Makes 8 servings

Prep. Time: 10 minutes ⚜ *Cooking Time: 1½–2 hours* ⚜ *Ideal slow cooker size: 6- or 7-qt.*

4 oz. unsweetened chocolate

¾ cup coconut oil

¾ cup frozen diced okra, partially thawed

3 large eggs

1 ½ cups xylitol or your choice of sweetener

1 teaspoon pure vanilla extract

¼ tsp. mineral salt

¾ cup coconut flour

½ –¾ cup coarsely chopped walnuts or pecans, optional

1. Melt chocolate and coconut oil in small saucepan.

2. Put okra and eggs in blender. Blend until smooth.

3. Measure all other ingredients in mixing bowl.

4. Pour melted chocolate and okra over the dry ingredients and stir with fork just until mixed.

5. Pour into greased slow cooker.

6. Cover and cook on high for 1½–2 hrs.

Per Serving (optional nuts not included in analysis)

Calories 421, Kilojoules 1761, Protein 8 g,
Carbohydrates 15 g, Total Fat 38 g, Saturated Fat 24 g,
Monounsaturated Fat 5 g, Polyunsaturated Fat 6 g,
Cholesterol 70 mg, Sodium 220 mg, Fiber 7 g

Tasty Tofu Brownie Snacks

Mary Ann Lefever, Lancaster, PA
Makes 9 servings

Prep. Time: 10–15 minutes ⚜ *Baking Time: 22 minutes* ⚜ *Cooling Time: 15 minutes*

1⅓ cups whole wheat pastry flour

½ tsp. baking soda

½ tsp. cinnamon

⅓ cup European-processed cocoa powder, unsweetened

¼ cup unsweetened applesauce

1 tsp. canola oil

½ cup honey

1 pkg. Mori-Nu Silken Lite Firm Tofu, drained

1 tsp. vanilla extract

2 Tbsp. chopped walnuts, optional, not included in analyses

1. Preheat oven to 350°.

2. Cut piece of waxed paper to fit in bottom of 8 × 8 baking pan. With paper removed, spray bottom and sides of pan with non-stick cooking spray. Place waxed paper on top of greased pan bottom and spray top of waxed paper.

3. In food processor fitted with metal chopping blade, process all dry ingredients (excluding walnuts). Empty into small bowl and set aside.

4. Place all wet ingredients in food processor and process until smooth, scraping bowl sides occasionally.

5. Add dry mixture all at once to wet ingredients in food-processor bowl.

6. Pulse to blend until dry ingredients are just moistened.

7. Scrape mixture into prepared pan. Sprinkle with nuts if you wish.

8. Bake for 22 minutes, or until brownies pull away from sides.

9. Let cool 15 minutes before cutting into squares.

Per Serving

Calories 138, Kilojoules 577, Protein 5 g,
Carbohydrates 28 g, Total Fat 1 g, Saturated Fat 0.3 g,
Monounsaturated Fat 0.4 g, Polyunsaturated Fat 0.3 g,
Cholesterol 0 mg, Sodium 104 mg, Fiber 3 g

Honey-Sweetened Spice Cake

Doyle Rounds, Bridgewater, VA
Makes 12 servings

Prep. Time: 15 minutes ❧ *Cooling Time: 20–30 minutes* ❧ *Baking Time: 25 minutes*

1 cup raisins
1 cup water
1⅓ cups unsweetened applesauce
2 eggs, beaten
2 Tbsp. honey
⅓ cup vegetable oil
1 tsp. baking soda
2 cups whole wheat pastry flour
1½ tsp. ground cinnamon
½ tsp. ground nutmeg
1 tsp. vanilla extract

1. In a saucepan, cook raisins in water until water evaporates.

2. Pour into mixing bowl and let cool.

3. When raisins are cool, stir in applesauce, eggs, honey, and oil. Mix well.

4. Blend in baking soda and flour.

5. Stir in cinnamon, nutmeg, and vanilla, blending well.

6. Pour into greased 8 × 8 baking pan.

7. Bake at 350° for 25 minutes, or until tester inserted in center of cake comes out clean.

Per Serving
Calories 172, Kilojoules 720, Protein 4 g,
Carbohydrates 29 g, Total Fat 5 g, Saturated Fat 0.5 g,
Monounsaturated Fat 3.5 g, Polyunsaturated Fat 1 g,
Cholesterol 0 mg, Sodium 126 mg, Fiber 3 g

Pumpkin Cupcakes

Katrina Smith, Sheldon, WI
Makes 24 servings

Prep. Time: 20 minutes ♣ *Baking Time: 15 minutes*

Egg substitute equivalent to 4 eggs
½ cup canola oil
¾ cup honey
2 cups pumpkin
3 cups whole wheat flour
2 tsp. cinnamon
3 tsp. baking powder
2 tsp. baking soda
¼ tsp. salt
1 tsp. ground ginger
1 cup raisins, optional, not included in analyses

1. In a large mixing bowl, beat egg substitute, oil, and honey together until frothy.

2. Stir in pumpkin.

3. In a separate bowl, combine dry ingredients, including raisins if you wish.

4. Slowly blend dry ingredients into wet ingredients.

5. Fill 24 individual cupcake papers ½–⅔ full.

6. Bake at 350° 15 minutes, or until toothpick inserted in centers of cupcakes comes out clean.

Per Serving

Calories 141, Kilojoules 590, Protein 3 g, Carbohydrates 21 g, Total Fat 5 g, Saturated Fat 0.5 g, Monounsaturated Fat 1.5 g, Polyunsaturated Fat 3 g, Cholesterol trace, Sodium 180 mg, Fiber 2.5 g

Morning Glory Cupcakes

Barb Harvey, Quarryville, PA
Makes 20 servings

Prep. Time: 15 minutes ⚘ *Baking Time: 18–22 minutes* ⚘ *Cooling Time: 5 minutes*

2 cups whole wheat flour
1 cup sugar
2 tsp. baking soda
2 tsp. ground cinnamon
2 cups shredded carrots
⅓ cup chopped dried apricots
⅓ cup sunflower kernels
⅓ cup flaked coconut
⅓ cup semi-sweet chocolate chips
2 medium-sized ripe bananas, mashed
Egg substitute equivalent to 3 eggs
½ cup vegetable oil
2 tsp. vanilla extract

1. In large mixing bowl, combine flour, sugar, baking soda, and cinnamon.

2. Add carrots, apricots, sunflower kernels, coconut, and chocolate chips.

3. Stir in mashed bananas.

4. In separate bowl, beat eggs, oil, and vanilla together.

5. Stir wet ingredients into carrot mixture just until moistened.

6. Fill 20 greased or paper-lined cupcake cups ⅔ full.

7. Bake at 375° 18–22 minutes, until tester inserted into centers of cupcakes comes out clean.

8. Cool 5 minutes. Remove from pans to wire racks.

Per Serving

Calories 193, Kilojoules 808, Protein 4 g,
Carbohydrates 28 g, Total Fat 8 g, Saturated Fat 2 g,
Monounsaturated Fat 2 g, Polyunsaturated Fat 4 g,
Cholesterol trace, Sodium 158 mg, Fiber 3 g

Strawberry Shortcake Cups

Joanna Harrison, Lafayette, CO
Makes 8 servings

Prep. Time: 20 minutes ❧ *Baking Time: 12 minutes* ❧ *Cooling Time: 7 minutes*

1 quart (4 cups) fresh strawberries

3 Tbsp. agave nectar,* or honey, divided

1 ½ cups whole wheat pastry flour

1 tsp. baking powder

⅛ tsp. salt

¼ cup trans-fat-free buttery spread

Egg substitute equivalent to 1 egg, or 2 egg whites

½ cup skim milk

1. Mash or slice strawberries in a bowl. Stir in 2 Tbsp. agave nectar. Set aside.

2. In a good-sized mixing bowl, combine flour, baking powder, salt, and 1 Tbsp. agave nectar.

3. Cut buttery spread into dry ingredients with pastry cutter or 2 knives until crumbly.

4. In a small bowl, beat egg substitute and milk together.

5. Stir wet ingredients into flour mixture just until moistened.

6. Fill eight greased muffin cups ⅔ full of batter.

7. Bake at 425° for 12 minutes, or until golden.

8. Allow cakes to cool in baking tins 7 minutes. Then remove from muffin cups to cool on wire rack.

9. Just before serving, split shortcakes in half horizontally. Spoon berries over cake halves.

* Note:

Agave nectar is a sweet, honey-like syrup made from the succulent cactus-like agave plant. You may substitute honey if you don't have agave nectar.

Per Serving

Calories 173, Kilojoules 724, Protein 5 g, Carbohydrates 26 g, Total Fat 6 g, Saturated Fat 1.5 g, Monounsaturated Fat 1 g, Polyunsaturated Fat 3.5 g, Cholesterol trace, Sodium 183 mg, Fiber 4 g

Extra Information

Abbreviations used in this cookbook

lb. = pound

oz. = ounce

pkg. = package

pt. = pint

qt. = quart

Tbsp. = tablespoon

tsp. = teaspoon

9 x 13 baking pan = 9 inches wide by 13 inches long

8 x 8 baking pan = 8 inches wide by 8 inches long

5 x 9 loaf pan = 5 inches wide by 9 inches long

Assumptions

flour = unbleached or white, and all-purpose

oatmeal or oats = dry, quick or rolled (old-fashioned), unless specified

pepper = black, finely ground

rice = regular, long-grain (not minute or instant)

salt = table salt

shortening = solid, not liquid

spices = all ground, unless specified otherwise

sugar = granulated sugar (not brown and not confectioners')

Equivalents

dash = little less than ⅛ tsp.

3 teaspoons = 1 Tablespoon

2 Tablespoons = 1 oz.

4 Tablespoons = ¼ cup

5 Tablespoons plus 1 tsp. = ⅓ cup

8 Tablespoons = ½ cup

12 Tablespoons = ¾ cup

16 Tablespoons = 1 cup

1 cup = 8 oz. liquid

2 cups = 1 pint

4 cups = 1 quart

4 quarts = 1 gallon

1 stick butter = ¼ lb.

1 stick butter = ½ cup

1 stick butter = 8 Tbsp.

Beans, 1 lb. dried = 2–2½ cups (depending upon the size of the beans)

Bell peppers, 1 large = 1 cup chopped

Cheese, hard (for example, cheddar, Swiss, Monterey Jack, mozzarella), 1 lb. grated = 4 cups

Cheese, cottage, 1 lb. = 2 cups

Chocolate chips, 6-oz. pkg. = 1 scant cup

Coconut, 3-oz. pkg., grated = 1 cup, lightly filled

Crackers, graham, 12 single crackers = 1 cup crumbs

Crackers (butter, saltines, snack), 20 single crackers = 1 cup crumbs

Herbs, 1 Tbsp. fresh = 1 tsp. dried

Lemon, 1 medium-sized = 2–3 Tbsp. juice

Lemon, 1 medium-sized = 2–3 tsp. grated rind

Mustard, 1 Tbsp. prepared = 1 tsp. dry or ground mustard

Oatmeal, 1 lb. dry = about 5 cups dry

Onion, 1 medium-sized = ½ cup chopped

Pasta: Macaronis, penne, and other small or tubular shapes, 1 lb. dry = 4 cups uncooked

Noodles, 1 lb. dry = 6 cups uncooked spaghetti, linguine, fettucine, 1 lb. dry = 4 cups uncooked

Potatoes, white, 1 lb. = 3 medium-sized potatoes = 2 cups mashed

Potatoes, sweet, 1 lb. = 3 medium-sized potatoes = 2 cups mashed

Rice, 1 lb. dry = 2 cups uncooked

Sugar, confectioners', 1 lb. = 3½ cups sifted

Whipping cream, 1 cup un-whipped = 2 cups whipped

Whipped topping, 8-oz. container = 3 cups

Yeast, dry, 1 envelope (¼ oz.) = 1 Tbsp.

Metric Equivalent Measurements

If you're accustomed to using metric measurements, I don't want you to be inconvenienced by the imperial measurements I use in this book.

Use this handy chart, too, to figure out the size of the slow cooker you'll need for each recipe.

Weight (Dry Ingredients)

1 oz		30 g
4 oz	¼ lb	120 g
8 oz	½ lb	240 g
12 oz	¾ lb	360 g
16 oz	1 lb	480 g
32 oz	2 lb	960 g

Slow Cooker Sizes

1-quart	0.96 l
2-quart	1.92 l
3-quart	2.88 l
4-quart	3.84 l
5-quart	4.80 l
6-quart	5.76 l
7-quart	6.72 l
8-quart	7.58 l

Volume (Liquid Ingredients)

½ tsp.		2 ml
1 tsp.		5 ml
1 Tbsp.	½ fl oz	15 ml
2 Tbsp.	1 fl oz	30 ml
¼ cup	2 fl oz	60 ml
⅓ cup	3 fl oz	80 ml
½ cup	4 fl oz	120 ml
⅔ cup	5 fl oz	160 ml
¾ cup	6 fl oz	180 ml
1 cup	8 fl oz	240 ml
1 pt	16 fl oz	480 ml
1 qt	32 fl oz	960 ml

Length

¼ in	6 mm
½ in	13 mm
¾ in	19 mm
1 in	25 mm
6 in	15 cm
12 in	30 cm

Index

About the Author

Hope Comerford is a mom, wife, elementary music teacher, blogger, recipe developer, public speaker, Young Living Essential Oils essential oil enthusiast/educator, and published author. In 2013, she was diagnosed with a severe gluten intolerance and since then has spent many hours creating easy, practical and delicious gluten-free recipes that can be enjoyed by both those who are affected by gluten and those who are not.

Growing up, Hope spent many hours in the kitchen with her Meme (grandmother) and her love for cooking grew from there. While working on her master's degree when her daughter was young, Hope turned to her slow cookers for some salvation and sanity. It was from there she began truly experimenting with recipes and quickly learned she had the ability to get a little more creative in the kitchen and develop her own recipes.

In 2010, Hope started her blog, *A Busy Mom's Slow Cooker Adventures*, to simply share the recipes she was making with her family and friends. She never imagined people all over the world would begin visiting her page and sharing her recipes with others as well. In 2013, Hope self-published her first cookbook, *Slow Cooker Recipes 10 Ingredients or Less and Gluten-Free*, and then later wrote *The Gluten-Free Slow Cooker*.

Hope became the new brand ambassador and author of Fix-It and Forget-It in mid-2016. Since then, she has brought her excitement and creativeness to the Fix-It and Forget-It brand. Through Fix-It and Forget-It, she has written *Fix-It and Forget-It Lazy & Slow, Fix-It and Forget-It Healthy Slow Cooker Cookbook, Welcome Home Cookbook, Fix-It and Forget-It Holiday Favorites, Fix-It and Forget-It Cooking for Two, Fix-It and Forget-It Crowd Pleasers for the American Summer, Fix-It and Forget-It Dump Dinners and Dump Desserts, Fix-It and Forget-It Instant Pot Cookbook, Welcome Home Diabetic Cookbook, Welcome Home Harvest Cookbook*, and more.

Hope lives in the city of Clinton Township, Michigan, near Metro Detroit. She's lived in Michigan her whole life. She has been happily married to her husband and best friend, Justin, since 2008. Together they have two children, Ella and Gavin, who are her motivation, inspiration, and heart. In her spare time, Hope enjoys traveling, singing, cooking, reading books, spending time with friends and family, and relaxing.

Also Available